# A Guide to...
# Popular
# Conures
## AS PET AND AVIARY BIRDS

*It is not only fine feathers that make fine birds. – Aesop*

*By Ray Dorge & Gail Sibley*

Published and Edited by ABK Publications ©

**First Published 2001 by
ABK Publications
PO Box 6288,
South Tweed Heads,
NSW. 2486. Australia.**

**ISBN 0 9577024 34**

**Front Cover:**
Top left: Crimson-bellied Conure.
Centre right: Janday Conure.
Bottom left: Queen of Bavaria's Conure.
Bottom right: Pair of Golden-crowned Conures.
**Back Cover:** Nanday Conure.
(All cover photographs by Peter Odekerken)

All other photographs by Gail Sibley
except where shown.

Design, Type and Art: PrintHouse Multimedia Graphics
Colour Separations: Splash Colour
Printing: Penfold Buscombe Pty Ltd

# CONTENTS

# WORDS OF ENCOURAGEMENT AND CAUTION

The study of conures in aviculture is in its infancy. Little has been recorded for posterity. Therefore, we encourage you to record your observations and to share them with others. Join bird societies, attend parrot conventions, symposiums and exhibitions. Become an active member of local parrot clubs. Become involved. Your input is needed.

A word of caution for potential breeders of conures. From the very start, avoid becoming overcommitted. Ensure that you have a viable, dependable outlet for your chicks before you initiate a breeding program. Without an outlet, the more prolific conure species will overrun you with chicks that will turn into adults having their own chicks – a self-perpetuating problem. Overcommitment can lead to disenchantment and possibly to loss of interest altogether.

For the conure fanatic who has already mastered the pitfalls of bird keeping, we challenge you to qualify your aviary for the Model Aviculture Program MAP. Certification in an avian training course would also be an admirable personal goal.

The **Certified Avian Specialist** (CAS) program, sponsored by the Pet Industry Joint Advisory Council (USA), consists of two parts each followed by an examination. Upon successful completion, a CAS certificate is awarded. The first section of the program consists of a four hour lecture/seminar. A home workbook/reference section follows. The program is designed to increase the knowledge and expertise of pet industry personnel who handle companion animals.

The **Model Aviculture Program** (MAP), established in 1990, was designed by American aviculturists and avian veterinarians to improve avicultural practices by the setting of basic standards for avian husbandry. A veterinarian completes the inspection following MAP guidelines.

B. SIBLEY

*The authors, Ray Dorge and Gail Sibley.*

# ABOUT THE AUTHORS

Ray Dorge and Gail Sibley have been keeping and breeding parrots ('far too many' according to their friends and relatives) for over 15 years. They have also had the privilege of being keepers for an aviary/sanctuary, co-owned and supervised by an avian veterinarian, that housed macaws, cockatoos, Amazon, African Grey and Hawk-headed Parrots and conures.

Ray Dorge is an author, columnist and freelance writer. Ray's column, *Squawks 'n' Chatter*, which appears in *Australian Birdkeeper* magazine and the column, *News and Views Stateside* appearing in *Parrots* magazine keep him on his avicultural toes. His aviculture and wildlife conservation articles appear regularly in Australia, the UK, Germany and the USA. Born and raised in Canada, he obtained his Bachelor's Degree (Anthropology focus) from Queen's University in Kingston, Canada.

Gail Sibley is a pastel and watercolour artist, as well as a freelance photographer. Her artwork is found in private and public collections worldwide. Born and raised in Kingston, Jamaica she completed her A-levels in England. She then went on to obtain a Bachelor's Degree in Fine Arts (Honours) from the University of Manitoba, Canada and a Masters Degree in Art History from the renowned Queen's University in Kingston, Canada. Gail's photography accompanies Ray's articles and appears in *A Guide to Pet & Companion Birds*, their first book together.

# ACKNOWLEDGEMENTS

Take note! If you should choose to skip this section you will miss the introductions to those busy avicultural professionals who so unselfishly contributed their insider secrets and qualified opinions.

## Rolling the Credits

'There is a tremendous need for information on conures as pets,' explained Janet Casagrande, of Rain Coast Aviary, Vancouver Island, Canada. Janet and Brian Casagrande thus seeded the idea for this book.

We then approached our Publisher, Nigel Steele-Boyce, with the proposal for this book. He gave us his approval and provided a list of popular conures currently available in Australia. We thank him for always being receptive to our ideas, for his confidence in us, and it goes without saying, for his patience and understanding during the writing process.

The Casagrandes breed a wide range of conures including some very rare species for which they are applying for First Breeding Awards in Canada. They generously loaned us many of their reference books on conures. This collection was the springboard for our research.

We are honoured that a renowned and highly respected aviculturist and author, Rosemary Low, allowed us to quote her descriptions of each of the species. Thank you very much Rosemary.

Sandra (Sandi) Brennan of Fine Feathered Flock Aviary who is the current President of the International Conure Association located in New Mexico, USA, was enthusiastic about our book. Not only did she offer her breeding experiences but also introduced us to other conure devotees. Sandi is no stranger to the ways of the conure. Bird keeping began at age six with two finches but did not take full flight until much later, when she was just married. Sandi and Martin Brennan caught what they call 'the fever,' while on honeymoon at Parrot Jungle in Florida, USA. They soon found themselves in the possession of over 200 birds ranging from finches to macaws. Since 1989, Martin has focussed on macaws, and Sandi on conures. The Brennans have over 30 conure species of which they have bred all but ten.

For an insight into a neighbourhood conure aviary, we visited Bob and Wendy Wilson who own Saxe Point Aviary in Victoria, Canada. Outdoor flights overlook their backyard gardens and indoor flights occupy the greater part of their walk-out basement. It comes as no surprise that pet parrots have colonised almost every room of their home. They have owned birds for 11 years. Currently, Saxe Point Aviary houses the Sun Conure *Aratinga solstitialis*, the Nanday Conure *Nandayus nenday* and the Maroon-bellied Conure *Pyrrhura frontalis*. Bob and Wendy's aviary motto is 'Healthy, happy adult birds breed happy, healthy babies.'

For a look at the business of conure breeding, we visited Judi Robben at Free Flyte Aviary in Kansas, USA. Judi, a registered nurse and paramedic, is also a certified avian specialist graduate and has qualified her aviary for MAP certification. 'I did both certifications as goals to improve my knowledge base and become more professional in my business.' She has vast experience with a variety of conures as they are her greatest love, the Painted Conure *Pyrrhura picta picta* being her favourite. Judi is a Founding Member of the Pyrrhura Breeders Association.

She introduced us to another Founding Member, Don Harris, who is currently serving as President of the Pyrrhura Breeders Association, for his impressions on his Fiery-shouldered Conures *Pyrrhura egregia*.

Another business minded, passionate conure breeder we have had the pleasure of meeting is June L. DiCiocco whose Hideaway Farm Aviary is in North Carolina, USA. Her aviary is also MAP certified. June specialises in the rare Queen of Bavaria's or Golden Conure *Guaruba guarouba*.

June introduced us to Kam Pelham-Polk, a Founding Member of the International Conure Association. Pelham-Polk's Conures and Company Aviary is a closed aviary in Houston, Texas, USA. Together with her husband and teenage daughter, Kam has been breeding birds for approximately 13 years and confesses to being totally addicted to the Sharp-tailed Conure *Aratinga acuticaudata acuticaudata*, specialising in them for the past five years.

We contacted Rick Jordan, renowned bird breeder, author and lecturer, for feedback on the Crimson-bellied Conure *Pyrrhura perlata perlata*. Rick is a partner in Hill Country Aviaries, Texas, USA that houses over 450 pairs of parrots of over 70 species – 18 of which are conure species and colour mutations. His facility participates in several Species Survival Plans and Studbooks, and has been awarded two US First Breeding Awards through the American Federation of Aviculture (AFA) Inc. He is a firm believer in the benefits of captive breeding and the supply and trade in captive-bred birds to reduce the pressures on wild flocks of the same species. He hopes that his work will someday have a direct and positive impact on the conservation of parrots in the wild. Currently Rick is the AFA CITES Committee Chairman where he monitors and provides input to the Convention pertaining to the keeping and trading of birds on a worldwide basis.

We also met with James and Patricia Taylor of Taylormade Aviaries in Victoria, Canada. James is currently elected in the positions of President of the Canadian Parrot Symposium West Society, President of the Avian Preservation Foundation, Vice-President of the Aviculture Advancement Council of Canada and President of the Vancouver Island Cage Bird Society. During the eight years James and Patricia have been parrot keeping, they have won a Canadian First Breeding Award.

To find out more about conures as companion birds, we interviewed Michael and Sue Yakubowich, Bryan Emery and Joanne Belanger. Sue Yakubowich did extensive research on various conures before deciding upon the Sharp-tailed Conure A. a. acuticaudata. She generously shared her conure toy-making tips and ideas. Bryan Emery, a very mature 14 year old who shows all the promise of becoming one of the next generation's great aviculturists, told us about his experiences with conures and other parrots. Joanne Belanger has worked in a parrot rescue station and is dedicated to the welfare of all captive parrots. She spoke of the need for parrot care information as she told us of her experiences. Everyone was very frank about the advantages and the disadvantages of having a house pet with the potential to arouse the wrath of the family and the neighbourhood.

We would also like to thank Julie Weiss Murad, Founder and current President of the Gabriel Foundation in Colorado, USA for her words of wisdom on parrot rescue and rehabilitation facilities; Michael Lockey, Director of Evergreen Acres Bird Sanctuary in Canada, for his quote on the Sharp-tailed Conure A. a. acuticaudata; Glenn Reynolds, primary fund-raiser for the World Parrot Trust-USA Golden Conure Survival Fund, for his look behind the scenes at the World Parrot Trust; Carmen LeComte at Pets Plus for a peek into the retail sales of conures; Joe Clemente for sharing his photographs and tales of the Patagonian Conure Cyanoliseus patagonus; and Alvaro Sanchez for his descriptions of the South American landscape.

Our thanks also go to fellow author Sylvia Sikundar for encouraging us during those times when the writing process sailed into doldrums.

And that brings us to Elizabeth Pellett, who has been behind the scenes all along, urging us to keep writing avicultural material for the sake of all parrots in captivity. We thank her for the opening quote by Aesop. Sadly, during the interval between the reading of our manuscript for our first book and the writing of this one, Elizabeth lost her cherished pet Galah Eolophus roseicapillus to an illness that could not be diagnosed. It was quite a blow. We therefore dedicate her quote to the loving memory of Rosie.

Sincere appreciation to Dr Bob Doneley BVSc MACVSc (Avian Health) for the information provided in the section Diseases and Disorders Common to Conures.

Both authors and publisher would like to sincerely thank Dr Terry Martin BVSc, author of A Guide to Colour Mutations and Genetics in Parrots, for the overview of colour mutations in conures and Australian aviculturist, author and photographer Peter Odekerken for supplying his superb photographs of the conure species discussed in this book.

Finally, our heartfelt thanks to Joanne and Jeremy Sibley for their unquestioning and unswerving love, support, and encouragement.

# INTRODUCTION

Dusky-headed
Conure

# PARTS OF A TYPICAL CONURE

(Illustration by R. Kingston)

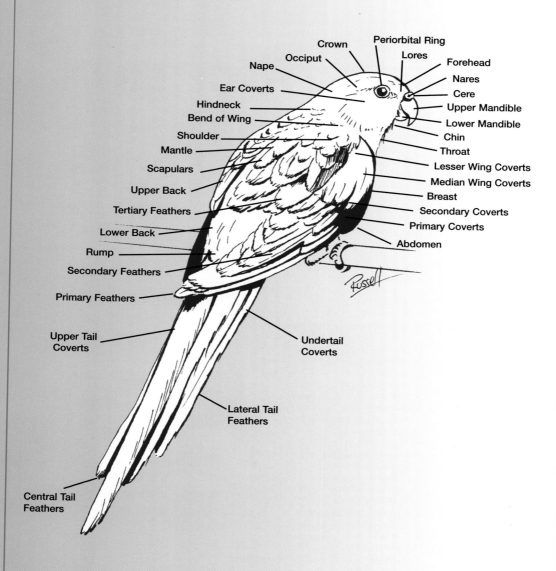

Crown
Periorbital Ring
Occiput
Lores
Forehead
Nape
Nares
Ear Coverts
Cere
Hindneck
Upper Mandible
Bend of Wing
Lower Mandible
Shoulder
Chin
Mantle
Throat
Scapulars
Lesser Wing Coverts
Upper Back
Median Wing Coverts
Tertiary Feathers
Breast
Lower Back
Secondary Coverts
Rump
Primary Coverts
Secondary Feathers
Abdomen
Primary Feathers
Upper Tail Coverts
Undertail Coverts
Lateral Tail Feathers
Central Tail Feathers

Conures are overlooked and underrated in aviculture with information on them scattered and localised. This is primarily because of their infamous and often exaggerated reputation as being loud and destructive birds. These negative generalisations often cause potential conure keepers to shy away from obtaining conures, especially on a continent such as Australia with its teeming and readily available supply of indigenous parrots. Having said that, there are 18 species of conure currently kept and bred in Australia.

This book aims to set the record straight on how delightful a pet, companion and aviary bird a conure really can be. It is time to bring this personable parrot to the forefront and thus, into the avicultural eye. It goes almost without saying, however, that it is not our intention to sell you on the idea of conure keeping unless you are already familiar with parrot keeping as a whole and all the responsibilities that entails.

Although researched and written in North America, all of the information relating to keeping and breeding conures can be readily applied to Australian conditions. In fact the Australian climate is extremely suitable for breeding conures.

Of the 18 species of conure kept in Australia at the time of publication, 15 of them require registration with the National Exotic Bird Registration Scheme (NEBRS). At the time of publishing, the exempt species are the Janday Conure *Aratinga jandaya*, the Sun Conure *Aratinga solstitialis* and the Nanday Conure *Nandayas nenday*. The numbers of each species of conure kept in Australia range from substantial to extremely low numbers.

We have restricted the scope of this book to the discussion of the more popular conures available in Australia and worldwide. Most of the species described herein are becoming popular throughout the world.

*Nanday Conure*
*(below shoulder level as recommended).*

This book is also intended for potential conure owners who are either looking for information on whether keeping conures is really for them or are attempting to make an informed decision on conure species selection, as well as for existing conure keepers who wish to broaden their knowledge.

Together we will discover how wild conures live in their native habitats and how captive conures are provided for in the artificial environments created by their keepers. We will also find out how conures endear themselves to their owners, making themselves irreplaceable as pets, companion birds or as aviary specimens.

For those of you already smitten by conures, we hope that the re-telling of other owners' experiences will enhance your understanding of your own conures, and thus make your conure keeping experience even more enjoyable.

Owners of conures do not seem to agree on which species of conure makes the best pet, the best companion or even the best aviary bird. Each owner we spoke with had their own particular favourite, and each had sound, logical reasoning for their choice. So you will have to make up your own mind.

Our wish is that this book will spark your interest to continue learning more about

*Maroon-bellied Conure in breeding cage.*

conures, as well as other parrot species. Please use this book as an encouragement to record your own experiences.

## Conure Classification Simplified

Conures come in two main genres: the *Aratinga* and the *Pyrrhura*. Each genus has its advantages and disadvantages.

A few other small groups exist. One genus, *Nandayus nenday*, counts the Nanday Conure as its sole member. Aviculturists are currently debating as to whether *Nandayus nenday* would be better placed amongst the ranks of *Aratinga*.

The Queen of Bavaria's Conure *Guaruba guarouba*, formerly a member of the *Aratinga* genus, was only recently granted its own genus, *Guaruba*.

The Patagonian Conure *Cyanoliseus patagonus patagonus*, is the other genus included in this book.

# CONURE BEHAVIOUR – SPECIAL CONSIDERATIONS

In this section you will find tips to help you to control your conure's destructiveness, keep its nippiness at bay, and accommodate these species' urgent need to be active and entertained. By taking a few moments now to understand something of your conure's behaviour, you can take steps to keep your ownership experience enjoyable and avoid potential annoyances from surfacing in the future.

### *Loudness*

By avicultural definition, a silent conure does not exist. Conures enjoy squawking, especially in the morning and the late afternoon. A conure's voice can easily reach a pitch way beyond the tolerance level of most neighbourhoods. However, some conure species are naturally quieter than others. Making a choice from those in the quieter *Pyrrhura* genus, by the way, will not guarantee that your conure will be any quieter than one selected from the representatives of the quietest of *Aratinga*. There are exceptions in both groups. So, when choosing a conure based on quiet or less harsh vocals, feel free to refer to the species findings made by avid conure keepers as listed in the Species section.

Kam Pelham-Polk discovered a simple method to stop her conures from squawking. She does this by talking to them and getting them into the talking mode. Kam believes that conures prefer to talk rather than squawk.

If your dream conure ranks with the loudest of all conures, Bob and Wendy Wilson have another solution. They suggest teaching your conures to whisper. The training of a loud conure to whisper takes a lot of patience and self-discipline. To begin with, you must refrain from raising your voice around your flock and speak only in whispers. Once your bird begins imitating your whispers, it should always be rewarded with verbal praise and a treat. Remember, a loud or noisy bird must be admonished in whispers also. Before long your conure will whisper its morning and evening calls, and especially when seeking your attention. For me, seeing was believing! The Wilsons' Nanday Conure cock is a superb whisperer. So yes, it can be done.

Naturally, the tamer the conure, the quieter it will be. No matter how much its species is known for loudness, an individual tame conure will be quieter because of its level of comfort with its surroundings. Thus, it will be less apt to resort to agitated chatter and unnecessary danger calls. Its song, however, will remain. When heard with an attitude of acceptance, those sounds will be held precious for their naturalness. Who can fault a conure for its cheerful calls, no matter how boisterous? At our aviary we close our eyes and enjoy our parrots' calls as if we are hearing them in the wild. We feel privileged, not annoyed.

If a conure's vocal intensity goes beyond your endurance level, instead of shouting back (your bird may think you are joining in the fun and be even more enthusiastic), go into another room and shut the door.

### Destructiveness

Conures do give their surroundings a good whittling, some more enthusiastically than others. Gnawing on something is a natural conure behaviour. However, this seemingly compulsive chewing behaviour becomes more than a nuisance when the conure begins to destroy valuable furnishings. Although it may be possible to train the bird to change its ways, this behaviour seems too deep-seated in conure behaviour to warrant the effort. The best way to deal with a 'gnawer' is to meet it on its own terms, by satisfying its natural instinct with ample, safe chewing materials.

Above: Dusky-headed Conure swinging on an electrical cord.
Below: Dusky-headed Conure decides to gnaw the electrical cord!

By restricting the roaming range of your conure, you will also restrict the area for potential destruction. By not giving a conure full liberty of your home, you protect your possessions from conure whittle damage. By allowing a bird free range in a home, a keeper inadvertently places the bird in mortal danger. Possible hazards include drowning in a water container such as an open toilet bowl, poisoning from nibbling on a 'suspicious' house plant and electrocution by gnawing on an electrical cord. By training your conure to stay on its playgym whenever it is out of its cage or flight and when not being handled, you will have the battle well under control.

### Nippiness

Conures do have a reputation for being nippy. Nipping behaviour can also be curbed and even stopped once its motivation is understood and the appropriate action taken. Nippiness in conures first surfaces when the birds pass from babyhood into adolescence, and then may reoccur during each breeding season. Some conures are more prone to nippiness at these times than others. However, some conures are no more nippy than the gentlest of parrots. As with other general conure characteristics, nippiness also varies with the individual.

*Left: Sun Conure chick learning to step up. Note that it uses its beak to climb. This is not to be discouraged as nipping behaviour.*

*Right: Sun Conure chick explores its environment with its beak. This is when you should teach your bird that fingers are off-limits.*

Youngsters, as well as adults, joust amongst themselves (and with their toys). These jousts include feigning a bite. If these sessions become serious, feathers may fly before one bird backs down. It is best not to encourage your bird to joust with you as this will undoubtedly lead to a misunderstanding. Therefore it is important that you never encourage a parrot to bite you.

Parrots also joust to test one another for top bird position over the flock, to ward off a rival or intruder, or to decide a new arrival's place in the flock. A human might therefore understand that a nippy conure is testing its keeper's mettle, under conure rules, of course. Knowing something of conure behaviour and parrot behaviour in general will assist you to understand your conure's instinctive motivation for being nippy.

Adhering to the following rules may assist in curbing nipping behaviour.

*Joanne Belanger with Gillie, a Nanday Conure, on her (off limits) shoulder.*

**Rule 1:** Handle your conures below shoulder level. The highest perched conure is in charge. All lower perchers are subordinate, and potentially vulnerable. A bird perched above shoulder level, therefore, may assume it has the right to rule the roost belonging to the human. For humans to curb such insurrection, they must avoid both shoulder perching their conure, and supplying it with high perches.

A shoulder-perched parrot, coincidentally, is a parrot which is out of its keeper's control. If the conure becomes startled or agitated, the keeper's face, eyes, neck and ears are at risk of a lunge and nip strike. Unexpected lunges can also occur when the bird is attempting to exert its will when wanting its own way. (Conures are generally quite wilful little creatures!)

**Rule 2:** To preserve your rule over your roost, you must take charge. Always play the part of the confident ruler while with your conure. Act with a positive attitude, exuding confidence and authority whenever you speak to your conure. By maintaining boundaries and keeping to the rules, you will avoid confusion as to who is in charge. This will assist you in safeguarding your authority.

*Above: One year old Sharp-tailed Conure at play with keeper. Do not encourage your conure to bite you even at play.*
*Below: One year old Sharp-tailed Conure, Oscar, nipping hand. This, too, must be discouraged.*

**Rule 3:** Handle your conure often. Carmen LeComte of Pets Plus (a retail pet store selling a wide range of conures for pets), reminds her customers to handle their conure regularly, if not daily, if they want to keep the bird handtame. 'There is a subtle variation between each species, some are more inclined to wildness than others,' she explains.

**Rule 4:** If your conure is still a chick or if you handraise conures, always discourage any nippiness. Often this behaviour is merely exploring and rarely painful. Nevertheless, discourage finger exploration by distracting the chick with a twig or toy.

Conures must be forgiven a bite, when they are startled or cornered. They too have a right to protect themselves. To avoid these types of nips, always make your presence known by speaking calmly to your bird whenever in its vicinity. By the way, when you do get nipped, as all parrot keepers do on occasion, do not take umbrage or feel rejected. (This may be easier said than done.) If you take the wrong attitude, you may begin to avoid handling your bird. Eventually, your conure will become neglected or may find itself confined to its cage, captive. It is better to attempt an understanding of why the conure nipped you in the first place. (Avoid physical violence or the bird may sustain an injury as well as suffer mental trauma, and may try to avoid your company.)

## Busy Bird Complex

When not preening or snoozing, conures are highly active birds. It appears that they just cannot sit still, always needing to be active. When not given an outlet to burn off all that energy, such parrots may resort to self-abuse, mutilating their feathers.

*Sharp-tailed Conure on playgym food dish.*

To satisfy that need to be busy, provide chewing materials and lots of opportunity to explore their environment. A constant supply of fresh chewing branches, lots of amusing conure toys and a playgym are all highly recommended.

*Above: Sharp-tailed Conure bathing.*
*Right: Sharp-tailed Conure all wet and had enough.*

## Avid Bathers

Conures are, by all indications, avid bathers. They seem to relish splashing about in water. Provide them with the opportunity to bathe regularly. A conure frolicking in its bath, by the way, is not only enjoying the benefits of its health spa for maintaining its fine plumage, but it can also be a source of amusement and joy to avid conure watchers. Often, a conure is stimulated to bathe merely by the sound of running water. (Perhaps this is an instinct harking back to the wild, a reaction to the sound of waterfalls or rainfall.) Many conure owners acknowledge that the kitchen sink is the best place to bath a conure. The owners will leave the tap running with a small, gentle continuous stream of water and allow their conure to run through it. Ensure that the spray of water is not heavy – a parrot can drown if water showers directly up its nostrils. Never use soap on a bird – it will remove all the natural oils necessary for perfect plumage.

## A Bird with Attitude

Conures are birds with a 'big' attitude. Although they are relatively small parrots, they often act as if they are the size of large macaws. Therefore, it is imperative that you take charge at all times. If the bird becomes confused (not knowing what you want) or frustrated (feeling it should be rewarded), this can lead to a nip. Always use verbal and/or hand signals whenever attempting to communicate with your feathered friend. All parrots are good at reading body language, so visual cues work just as well as voice commands. By always using the 'Up' verbal command in an authoritative manner, your bird will learn to respond spontaneously, without hesitation. This can prove very handy when dealing with a rebellion or should hostilities break out in your flock.

Knowing all this, by the way, will not guarantee that your bird will never attempt to usurp your authority. Simply do not stand for it. Remain adamant or your bird will take charge, and much of the pleasure you derive from conure keeping will be lost.

Allow this brief introduction to whet your appetite to delve deeper into the study of your conure's behaviour and personality. Consider our information as the foundation upon which to base your study. For more on parrot behaviour and its interpretation, refer to *A Guide to Pet & Companion Birds*, ABK Publications.

# OBTAINING A CONURE

Where do you launch your quest for a conure? How do you negotiate the purchase? Offered here, in random order, are a few ideas for commencing a search. Herein too, is an introduction to avicultural etiquette to make your journey more pleasurable, less intimidating, and not at all embarrassing. For example, are you aware that it is considered quite rude to show up uninvited at the front door of an aviary?

Once you have completed your research and have decided upon a conure that you just cannot live without, it is time to embark on the hunt.

## How-to-Seek Methods

Fortunately for the prospective conure keeper as well as the conure species, captive breeding has established a stronghold in aviculture. Feel free to cancel the expedition to the wilds of South America, but do not abandon the idea of going on a hunt. Parrot breeders are a secretive group (for reasons that will become apparent) and you will have to flush them out.

Beating the bushes for a conure breeder is best undertaken using the 'Locating an Aviary' method. This relies on a lot of luck and the cooperation of others. Alert the sales manager of every bird supply store you come across.

*Nanday Conure exhibiting all the signs of a healthy bird, sitting on its cage.*

Avian veterinarian clinics are another good source for assistance. Briefly state your goal, namely to make contact with a local breeder or owner of conures. Offer your name and particulars for any of their clients to contact you. (Respect that the retailer and the veterinarian will want to keep their clients' business confidential, so avoid asking for names and addresses.)

Do not be surprised if this method proves fruitless in raising responses. Bird breeders and aviary owners often choose not to open their aviary to the general public as this would place their flock at risk of infection, or possible theft. A word of caution: resist resorting to knocking on aviary doors. A bothered breeder may prove to be very uncooperative, perhaps even hostile. Advice on proper avicultural etiquette will be provided a little later.

If you should, however, make contact with a parrot breeder or parrot owner, ask for directions to the conure you seek. Undoubtedly, someone will know someone else who breeds them. (Avid aviculturists generally like to know who has what.) Inquire about the existence of a local conure association, of parrot keeping clubs and of bird shows. A referral will open a lot of doors.

If perchance you are invited into a breeder's aviary or breeding facility, be thoughtful to observe the proper customs during the visit.

Many conures, especially those of the genus *Aratinga*, are often placed with parrot welfare organisations such as a rescue and rehabilitation facility. Julie Weiss Murad, Founder and current President of the Gabriel Foundation in Colorado, USA says that people often mistake a conures' nip as 'aggressiveness' or find its vocalisations unacceptable, and therefore the bird is discarded. A *bona fide* rescue and rehabilitation organisation has many parrots, that through no fault of their own, are in need of a loving and accepting home. If you visit a rescue/rehabilitation facility, Murad recommends that you be observant and ask many questions, taking the following points into consideration:

- The birds should appear to be well taken care of and be in good condition.
- Eyes should be bright.
- Nares should be clean.
- Feathers should be lustrous.
- Birds should seem healthy and alert.
- Husbandry should appear to be sound.

Feel confident that the organisation in question has:

- A strong education program.
- A structured adoption policy which takes time to match a bird to a human/family.
- Appropriate legal documentation regarding the legal guardianship/ownership of the conure and any stated follow-up procedures.
- The bird's file should include an appropriate social history (from the previous owner if possible) and/or details about its entry into the facility including a comprehensive veterinary examination. The file should also contain a chart of its weight, the caretaker's physical observations, the bird's diet and its likes and dislikes, etc.

Murad stresses that by asking lots of questions about the conure's interaction with staff, volunteers and other birds, you will get a fairly good understanding of that bird's particular personality. If you obtain a conure from a facility you must then allow the bird

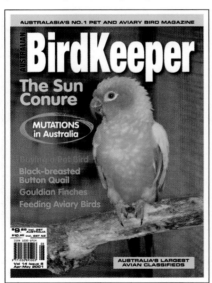

plenty of time to adjust to its new home, schedule and companions. Establishing a relationship built on patience, mutual trust and respect, kindness and consistency will provide you with a wonderful companion deserving of a lifetime of love.

Another point of departure for your conure quest could be to launch into the 'Research' method. (This procedure is the favourite of experienced parrot hunters.) Study the advertisements in parrot keeping publications such as *Australian Birdkeeper* magazine, and make the appropriate contacts. Also consider initiating an internet search, starting perhaps with the appropriate links on *ABK Publications'* own web site www.birdkeeper.com.au

Having left the 'Retail Purchase' method to the last does not imply that it should be considered a last resort. Many bird shops are owned and run by well qualified and experienced avian personnel.

Some even have their own aviary or breeding facilities. For an assessment of the shop, determine its level of conure parrot expertise and watch to see how their birds are handled, housed and maintained.

When you have finally cornered the conure of your choice, have the bird examined by an avian veterinarian before calling an end to the hunt.

## Avicultural Etiquette

As may already be apparent, we aviculturists are a strange lot. Not only do we speak using scientific terminology and keep very secretive about the location of our flocks, but we also have our own customs or etiquette.

For example, without proper introduction, undoubtedly you will receive a cool reception by an aviary owner or bird breeder until your purpose becomes clear. One reason for this is that private parrot 'jungles' are often targets for people wanting to entertain their children, to 'take the kids to see the parrots', and for those only seeking amusement. Unfortunately, parrot aviaries can also be the target for thieves. These are avicultural occupational hazards. Therefore, when making telephone contact with an aviary or breeding facility owner, quickly reassure them that your intentions are honourable and that the purchase of a conure is your goal.

*The chicks-for-sale area at Rain Coast Aviary offering Dusky-headed Conures at 10 weeks of age and Fiery-shouldered Conures at five months of age.*

While on a visit to an aviary or breeding facility, keeping your hands in your pockets or behind your back is considered good form. Resist touching anything including cages, bird toys and especially the birds. Wait until you are invited to do so. Every aviary intrusion places the entire flock at risk of infection. Who knows if the visitor has just stopped off at the local bird store or poultry farm and touched, even if unknowingly, a sick animal?

Some aviary and breeding facility owners insist on smocks and a change of foot gear (or a walk through a disinfectant foot bath) on their premises. The truly dedicated breeding facility often has a quarantine room where visitors must look through windows to view the aviary.

If you are invited to touch a bird, immediately volunteer to wash your hands. After a thorough hand-scrub, rinse and dry your hands well before proceeding to handle the bird. If you are offered a selection of birds to choose from, offer to repeat the hand-scrubbing process between individual birds.

Do not expect to get a 'good deal' just because you are negotiating directly with the breeder.

*Handraised Sun Conure at 6 1/2 months of age on playgym.*

## Conure Considerations

Here are some steps to follow when winding down the hunt.

Be sure that the bird you are considering is the exact species you seek. Unless you are completely familiar with the species, familiarise yourself with the information in this book to avoid confusion.

Be sure that the bird will survive its transition into your care. Is it old enough to feed on its own? Has it been fully weaned? Do not let an unscrupulous breeder – we hesitate to insinuate the existence of such a beast – catch you unaware. Unless you are well-versed in handrearing procedures, avoid acquiring birds that are not fully weaned. Handfeeding and weaning are tricky processes no matter what the salesperson may say to the contrary. Handfeeding is not a requirement for bonding with your bird.

*Handling a Conure: A Maroon-bellied Conure being held for examination. Parrots seem more at ease when grasping something, in this instance, its handler's right index finger. The conure's head is being held securely between the left index finger (holding top of head) and thumb (holding lower mandible). Note that the bird is being held so that its chest (and breathing) will not be restricted. Also note the closed band for identification.*

Be aware of the overall appearance of the pet store or breeder's aviary. Ask yourself if it is clean, whether the birds have ample food and clean water and whether all the birds appear healthy, lively and happy. An unhealthy environment may prove to be the cause of an illness that may only surface later, after you have had the bird in your possession for some time.

The bird must appear healthy, alert, bright-eyed, and active, have a clear vent and be in good feather. In nature, birds must always appear to look healthy, even if they are not. If birds display any sign of weakness or illness, a predator will pick them out. Therefore, if you are not experienced in assessing a bird's visual health, take along someone who is. Beforehand, familiarise yourself with what to look for. Dr. Michael Cannon's *A Guide to Basic Health & Diseases in Birds, ABK Publications,* is an excellent resource.

Ensure that your bird has adequate identification in case you are called upon to prove its provenance. It is important to be able to prove that the bird was not illegally imported. The bird should be properly banded with a closed, numbered leg band or be otherwise identifiable (perhaps with a microchip implant or a tattoo). Ask for a breeding pedigree certificate and a complete sales receipt. If your goal is to breed the conure, the bird's lineage will be necessary to ensure against inbreeding. In Australia it will be necessary to register with the National Exotic Bird Registration Scheme (NEBRS) for some species of conure.

If the conure looks healthy and meets your requirements as a pet or aviary bird, and, in short, you find you are smitten with the parrot and must own it immediately, resist the temptation to close the deal before obtaining a clearance from an avian veterinarian. The cost of the examination, of course, must be borne by you. It is like having insurance. After all, you would not buy a used car without having it checked over by a mechanic, would you? (Determine beforehand the veterinarian's fees, and specify that you require blood tests to be done. The laboratory costs will pay dividends in future peace of mind.)

If you are looking for a specific sex, make sure your bird comes with surgical or DNA sexing papers or is microchipped and check that the identification number on the document matches the number on the bird's leg band or microchip. As conure hens and cocks look alike (they are monomorphic), it is difficult, if not impossible, to tell them apart visually. Sexing is necessary. Do not rely on guesswork or you may face heartbreak and frustration later.

PELHAM-POLK

Before placing your hard-earned cash on the table, determine the return policy. You may have an allergy to conures or, more realistically, you or your neighbours may not be able to cope with the new sound intensity in your home or aviary. Many breeders maintain a no-return policy once a bird has left their aviary (especially when the purchaser has other birds from which the new bird may contract disease). To bring a bird back into an aviary would

*Kam Pelham-Polk with a four year old Patagonian Conure that is a lovable clown.*

mean placing their other birds at risk.

## A Conure Chick or an Adult?

Which has the potential to become the better conure pet or conure aviary bird: a chick or an adult bird? A just-weaned conure chick offers the growing up stage of babyhood, undoubtedly the most playful phase of bird life when exploring is at its peak. Making this choice, however, means that the new owner will have to be prepared to see the bird through adolescence into adulthood.

*Dusky-headed Conure chick at 10 weeks of age.*

An adult conure, on the other hand, will have gone through puberty. If it has been handreared but not handled since weaning, chances are it will be tame in an aviary but not tame as a companion bird without some effort. However, do not discount an adult conure just yet. Many adult birds are handled regularly and thus have remained tame. Some may even be just as playful as they were as a chick. More to the point, the adult parrot will have settled down, its personality will be established – what you see will be what you get. Although a just-weaned chick is often regarded as the best bird to acquire, an adult bird may have just as much to offer. (For more information on parrot adolescent behaviour, refer to *A Guide to Pet & Companion Birds, ABK Publications*.)

## Have Bird-Carrier, Will Travel

Now that you have bought your conure, how will you get it home? That is but one instance when owning a bird-carrier will prove beneficial. A carrier is very handy for a number of transporting reasons.

Some bird-carriers are specifically made for conure-sized parrots and are available from most bird supply retailers. A small animal carrier fitted with a dowel perch or a branch of eucalyptus or willow will also work just as well. Be sure that the carrier fits the bird: too large and the bird will be nervous in strange surroundings, too small and the bird will feel cramped and uncomfortable. As long as the perch is low enough to allow the bird to sit upright comfortably, without hitting the top of its head, and no feathers protrude from the carrier, the size should prove ideal for short trips. Toss in some apple chunks and your bird has a thirst-quenching in-transit meal on hand. For longer journeys, a food dish and water bottle, which is accessible to the bird, must be attached within the carrier.

A bird-carrier cover such as a large beach towel comes in handy as a way of calming the bird by blocking out unfamiliar terrain. As well, it stops draughts from chilling the traveller. (Draughts are one of the leading killers of captive birds.)

## New Acquisitions

If you have other birds, we recommend that you quarantine your new arrivals. This is a necessary precaution, because your other birds are at risk of contracting a contagious disease. Birds can carry diseases that only make the bird sick when the bird is under stress. Since moving house is stressful to birds, the first few weeks of settling in – when the conure is getting used to you, its new environment and a new routine – is the time when a bird may succumb to any diseases it is carrying. If it does get sick, you have protected the rest of your flock from anything contagious. If it does not get sick, then obviously you either have a bird that is not carrying any diseases, or one that is healthy enough to overcome any affliction it might be carrying.

A spare room or a second bathroom make excellent quarantine observation wards, especially when they offer fresh air from the outdoors and/or an exhaust fan to clear the room of airborne, disease-carrying bird dust.

A second bathroom is ideal as it may have its own plumbing for bird dish washing and cage cleanups. Wearing a separate smock and footwear in the observation ward is the aviculturist's first line of defence against accidentally carrying diseases out to other birds in the collection. For the same reason, antibacterial hand-scrubs are mandatory upon entering and exiting the quarantine area.

We recommend a minimum quarantine period of at least four weeks but suggest six weeks or more. The longer the better is our motto. Your avian veterinarian can offer guidance and should be consulted immediately if you see any change in the conure's appearance or behaviour. See Diseases and Disorders Common to Conures, page 37. For more information, refer to *A Guide to Basic Health and Disease in Birds* by Dr Michael Cannon, *ABK Publications*.

Although these precautions may seem extreme, to avoid having regrets later, it really does pay to be cautious.

# HUSBANDRY

*Sun
Conure*

Husbandry is another name for a labour of love, that is keeping your conures healthy and living a stress-free life. Although many conure needs are similar, differences arise according to species as well as to the way they are housed. Keeping a single house pet conure, for example, is quite different from housing mated pairs in a breeding facility. This section reveals what keepers have found to be the basic needs for the keeping of all conures under each of the housing situations. For ease of reference, this section is divided into three headings: Housing, What's on the Conure Menu?, and Entertaining Conures.

*Golden-crowned Conure.*

*Housing* describes conure accommodation whether your bird is kept as a house pet or an aviary specimen. Discussion of the design and actual construction aspects of an aviary or flight have been omitted in favour of more detailed information on providing for a conure as a pet bird. (*The Handbook of Birds, Cages & Aviaries, ABK Publications* contains information on flight and aviary design and assembly.)

*What's on the Conure Menu?* covers the food requirements of a conure which is similar for both an indoor pet and a bird kept in an outdoor aviary flight.

Conures, being the inquisitive and playful creatures they are, need entertainment to keep them from becoming bored. This holds for both the conure in a flight and the indoor pet. Although your companionship provides much entertainment for a single pet, when you are not available, your pet needs something to occupy its time. The same applies to the aviary bird that may have another bird for company. Nevertheless, a little extracurricular activity would not go amiss as you will read in *Entertaining Conures*.

# HOUSING

An aviary, a flight, a breeding facility and an indoor cage are all potential places for avicultural pride. Let us define some terms first.

An aviary is a general term describing an enclosure that houses birds. On the other hand, a flight describes something more specific: it is, in effect, a caged area with ample space for a captive bird to fly about – hence the name. A breeding facility is, obviously, a place where birds are bred. It may consist of flights as well as breeding cages. Because of the term 'facility', this type of setup assumes a number of pairs are in a breeding situation. An indoor cage is basically a home for your pet conure and can range from a standard minimum size to a large structure complete with all the mod cons.

## Flight Construction Materials

Regardless of whether you want a simple or a grand structure, the construction materials will be similar. Creation of your own conure flight or aviary can be an enjoyable experience – one of the thrills of aviculture. Fine tuning to give your birds as natural an environment as possible is the goal. All the conure owners we spoke with during our research were proud to display their aviaries. Their planning and construction were considered an ongoing achievement.

Brian Casagrande, whose Rain Coast Aviary houses a large cross-section of conures of various sizes, recommends 25mm x 12.5mm aviary wire mesh as the most appropriate size for the housing of all conure species. Casagrande says that when he tried the 25mm x 25mm mesh, it proved too large and would neck-trap smaller conures.

Select wire or cage bars of appropriate gauge that will match the strength of a much larger parrot with a forceful beak. Conures have amazingly strong beaks for their size. Remember to treat new and freshly cut wire, to prevent heavy metal poisoning, also known as 'new wire' disease. (Consult your avian veterinarian for a procedure to do this. Our avian veterinarian suggests vigorously scrubbing new wire, freshly cut wire and hardware with vinegar.)

Design your flight and aviary so that timber surfaces are protected from the gnawing beaks of your conures. The use of steel framing is recommended.

*Nanday Conures in aviary flight. Note how the timber is protected with cage wire.*

In Australia many conure breeders have chosen 12.5mm x 12.5mm aviary wire mesh of a fairly robust 13 gauge. This assists in rodent and snake protection of the birds. It is also commonplace after a vinegar scrub and hose down to paint the wire with an oil based acrylic paint of a dark colour, ie black or dark green. Not only does this prevent, to some degree, the possibility of the birds' exposure to heavy metal poisoning, it also allows the keeper to see the birds far more clearly.

*Author with Wendy Wilson at Saxe Point Aviary. Example of how conures are housed in outdoor flights in a neighbourhood.*

## Basic Aviary Design

Ideally, your flight will consist of an outdoor flight attached to an enclosure wherein your conure can take refuge from the elements: the wind, the heat, the cold and the damp. The best design allows retention of heat and escape of cold air in cold weather and vice versa during hot periods. In addition to proper insulation, consider the access size between the enclosure and the outdoor flight. In colder climates it is best to keep its size to a bare minimum. A closing device over the access helps with insulation and with isolation of an area to confine the residents, should this be required.

## Is Heating Necessary?

The golden rule for conure keeping where the birds have access to the outdoors is to maintain the indoor area above freezing. This obviously is directed to breeders in colder climates and not necessarily to Australasian aviculturists. If that means heating is necessary, then so be it. A roosting box provides added protection.

As winter approaches, your outdoor-housed conure will have had time to acclimatise naturally, through the change in seasons, to cooler overnight temperatures. Nature will have endowed your bird with extra warmth capacity from new feathers and heavier down.

## Acclimatising Your Conure

Many conures prove quite cold hardy, capable of acclimatising to a seasonal lifestyle. However, before you release your bird into an outdoor flight, know that doing so without taking proper precautions places your bird's health and its life at risk. Unlike a bird that has had this opportunity to acclimatise naturally, a new addition, or one that has been kept indoors all year, will be unprepared physiologically to endure chilly temperatures. These birds are best housed indoors over the winter months.

Never move an indoor conure into an outdoor aviary in the autumn. It is much better to wait for late spring/early summer, when indoor and outdoor temperatures are quite similar, and evening temperatures are not that much cooler than daytime temperatures. As prime feather condition is essential to insulate your conure against a chill, assist your bird to produce and maintain its own best insulation by providing a nutritious diet, a clean home and a bath at regular intervals. You and I may not be enamoured with the idea of bathing in the great outdoors during the height of winter, but we have seen our parrots splashing about in full glee even on very crisp mornings.

## Conure Breeding Facilities

We will look at two examples of conure breeding facilities. Both are highly regarded in the conure breeding world. The Casagrande's Rain Coast Aviary, in Canada, boasts the rare Fiery-shouldered Conure *Pyrrhura egregia*. June DiCiocco's aviary is home to the Queen of Bavaria's or Golden Conure *Guaruba guarouba*. Both aviaries are also designed to house a wide selection of different conure species.

Rain Coast Aviary's conure breeding pairs are set up in cages measuring 61cm square x 107cm long. Each has a nestbox measuring 23.5cm square x 35.5cm deep with a 6.5cm diameter entrance hole.

DiCiocco's conure breeding facility is Model Aviculture Program (MAP) certified. Breeding cages measure 61cm square x

*Breeding cage and nestbox for housing Dusky-headed Conures. The note card is a good idea for recording the number of eggs laid, hatch dates and general observations.*

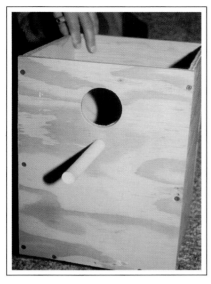

Above:
*Conure roost/nestbox interior at Rain Coast Aviary.*
Left:
*Conure roost/nestbox exterior at Rain Coast Aviary.*

122cm long. The nestbox measures 45cm square x 61cm deep. DiCiocco hastens to emphasise that a roost/nestbox of 30.5cm square x 61cm deep is better suited for the larger conures such as the Queen of Bavaria's Conure. (For details on specific conure species roost/nestbox requirements refer to the individual species.) By the way, DiCiocco's tip for increasing nestbox longevity is to use an ABS (hard plastic) nestbox measuring 20cm square x 55.8cm long for conures such as the Sun Conure *Aratinga solstitialis* and the Dusky-headed Conure *Aratinga weddellii* that chew their way out of timber nestboxes.

## A Conure's Private Residence – Its Cage

A cage is often interpreted as being a place of confinement. However, I prefer to think of my parrots' cages as their private playgrounds and residences wherein they may lay claim to and defend a territory. In my mind, a cage only becomes a prison when the parrot is not offered lots of out-of-cage experience on a regular basis, whether on a playgym or with its keeper.

What size of residence is best for your conure? Naturally, the bigger the better. Be careful to select a strongly built cage. Do not let the smallish size of conures deceive you. Commercial conure cages are made to withstand the abuse of strong beaks, even those of much larger parrots. Be careful to select a cage with the correct bar spacing. Strong cages are usually constructed for the larger parrots, so the cage bar spacing can be too wide and potentially are a neck-trapping hazard for birds the size of conures.

*A Sharp-tailed Conure preening on a playgym.*

Ease of cleaning is another factor to consider when making a cage selection. A cage which is too heavy to lift off its bottom for cleaning, or so large that it must be dismantled before moving for washing, may prove a burden on its owner and thus tend to become neglected. It cannot be stressed enough how important cleanliness is to a bird's health. That, along with an adequate diet, exercise and your companionship (or that of another bird) will help keep your conure healthy and happy.

Cages should always be rectangular (never circular) and constructed with a majority of horizontal bars (for ease of climbing). A cube-configured cage intended for housing cockatiels offers the necessary bar strength but is the very minimum size to house a conure. A plentiful supply of unsprayed branches, such as willow or eucalyptus, for gnawing and renewing perches should be available at all times.

A word of caution: avoid perches and perch covers that are made with sandpaper. They are sold as an aid to keeping your bird's toenails blunt. In effect, they are more harmful than

*Dusky-headed Conures in a commercially available conure cage.*

helpful. Not only can the sandpaper particles irritate the bird's feet, but the particles can be dangerous if digested. For toenail maintenance and as a beak wipe, it is better to choose a 'concrete' perch made of mineral stone and place it strategically somewhere along your conure's path to its food dishes (not where it would perch).

## 'Interior Design' – Conure Residence Style

You have just purchased a brand new conure cage or flight. It came with an assortment of accessories and, of course, absolutely no instructions about where to locate them. Following are some hints on setting up a conure cage, flight or breeding cage.

The nestbox is best positioned high as birds generally prefer to roost on the highest perch. Place it near the back of the cage, away from where food and water are located.

*Nanday Conure (with food in beak) on cage containing toys.*

Now for the food and water dishes. Are you left-handed or right-handed? Wait, don't laugh! It really does matter. You will want to service your cage in the way most comfortable for you. Do not make your reaches into the cage awkward, placing yourself at peril. Water and food dishes should be kept away from under branches, perches and swings to prevent fouling. When placing the perches, make sure to leave enough space for your parrot to flap its wings.

## Conure Cage Placement

Parrot keepers often put more thought into the positioning of a flight as it relates to their yard, than they do to the positioning of a conure cage in their home. The cage thus ends up being placed haphazardly, perhaps even in an unhealthy location for the birds.

A highly inquisitive or tame conure, for example, would naturally prefer to reside close to where the action is in its keeper's home, whereas its shyer cousin would probably choose to live a little further away with more privacy.

Consider giving your conure a cage with a view, be it a landscape or a humanscape. The cage must have a shady area out of direct sun, with a refuge from cold draughts. This will go a very long way towards keeping your conure healthy, since draughts are known to lower a bird's resistance to illness. Be aware also of the cold draught off a cold, closed window – a cage cover and a nestbox will offer some protection.

## Practical Cage Accessories

A conure cage cover, to cover part of the cage during the day and to cover it fully at night, is recommended. Not only does a cage cover stop draughts and offer shade in a sunny location, but it also seems to give the bird a feeling of security: it does not have to constantly monitor the sky overhead for predators. A cage cover also works to delay the dawn and in so doing, your conure's early morning calls. Select a cover made of a non-frayable fabric or your bird will inevitably find an opportunity to become entangled in loose threads. Choose a pattern and colour that does not frighten the inhabitant of the cage.

C-links, horse hasps and even padlocks are recommended for pet conure owners.

Along with the cage and its cover, another important cage accessory is a bird bath. Most conures relish bathing and will do so at every given opportunity.

If you value keeping your conure safe within its cage during its cage time, it would be wise to attach locking devices on all cage openings including doors and food dish access. Conures are escape artists and can quickly find their way into mischief when on the loose. Depending on how ingenious your bird is at opening the device, C-links, horse hasps and even padlocks are recommended by conure owners.

Most conures show a preference for roosting in an enclosed area at night, or when seeking privacy away from the hustle and bustle of everyday life. Timber, metal and ABS (hard plastic) nestboxes are commercially available. Some conure keepers provide a fabric tent style roost designed for hanging in a cage. These are often referred to as bird condominiums. Apparently, conures readily accept their parrot tent and will spend hours playing and hiding in it, as well as roosting in it.

## The Roost

For a conure, settling in means becoming familiar with its new surroundings and securing a roost. Conures, unlike many other parrots, generally favour a nestbox or log for this purpose. This holds true for conures housed in flights or cages. (For specifics refer to the section on individual species for the roost type and dimensions best suited to your conure.)

If the box you choose is made of timber, it should be natural and non-toxic. (Consult an avian veterinarian when unsure of the toxicity of the wood in your area.) The vapours given of by the glues used in laminated woods, such as plywood, are believed to be

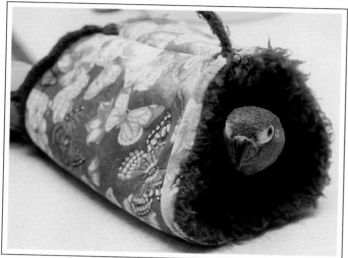

harmful to humans let alone to birds!

Depending on how destructive your conure is, having a store of timber or fabric roosts, will prove to be a time-saver in the long run.

Kam Pelham-Polk of Conures and Company Aviary believes that a single bird should be given something to sleep in at night that is small in size, to give the bird a secure feeling. Once adjusted to one, they seem to relish

*Above: Dusky-headed Conure trying out a bird tent.*
*Right: Maroon-bellied Conure in bird tent roost.*

sleeping in it.

When determining where you will place the roost, remember that conures are reclusive sleepers. To provide peace and quiet, position the roost entrance high and away from where food and water are served. This position should suit your conure provided, of course, that it is not one of those conure species that enjoys setting up roost in tunnels under your aviary floor. Fortunately, those species too will often make do with a more traditional roost.

# WHAT'S ON THE CONURE MENU?

To avoid relating only an ideal diet, observations were made on site, at a few conure breeding facilities. All the conure keepers surveyed are avid aviculturists and, valuing their birds' well-being, are very careful about what they feed their birds.

What came as a surprise to me was the inclusion of a seed mix in addition to the pelleted food being fed to conures. This proved to be standard practice. In addition, almost everyone fed their conures twice daily (in the morning and mid-afternoon). The pellets being offered were always a top quality brand and were always available to the birds. Water dishes were serviced at each feeding (twice a day or more depending on the aviary inspection routine).

## Vitamins, Minerals and Supplements

Some conure breeders regularly offer their birds cuttlefish bones (attached on the inside of the cages) and admitted to adding a calcium supplement to the bird's water once a month or so. Other breeders offered calcium supplements instead of cuttlefish bone. Although everyone supplemented their conures' diet with seed mix, none offered their birds grit. James Taylor of Taylormade Aviaries summed up our findings best when he stated 'From my understanding, there is no need to offer grit, and it can be harmful, causing impacted crop. Using corncob bedding or walnut hulls on the bottom of cages have also caused crop impaction.'

With regard to the necessity for vitamin and mineral supplements, Taylor explained that, if birds eat a good brand of pellets, then supplements are not recommended and in fact, can be detrimental. If the birds are not fed pellets, then supplements are recommended. Cuttlebone is offered, as it can do no harm. Many hens will eat it if they are laying.

June DiCiocco of Hideaway Farm Aviary does not offer her conures cuttlefish bone or any other mineral or vitamin supplements except for a liquid calcium syrup during the breeding season.

Judi Robben of Free Flyte Aviary, does use a mineral/vitamin amino acid

*Prepared fresh food, cut up and in dishes.*

*Saxe Point Aviary food mix.*

supplement, sprinkled very lightly on the soft foods. Supplements are not added to the water. Cuttlebone is available to all birds at all times. During the breeding season, if the hens are laying, she sprinkles a ground calcium supplement on the soft foods.

Sandi Brennan of Fine Feathered Flock Aviary keeps a mineral block in her conure cages at all times. She makes her own from plaster of Paris, vitamin/mineral powder and natural food colouring. During the breeding season she also sprinkles a commercial powder (vitamin D, calcium and phosphorus supplement and other minerals) on their cooked beans or other soft foods. Calcium is sometimes added to the water during the breeding season. Although her conures are fed seed, they are not offered grit, as the seeds are digested completely without it (in a healthy bird).

Don Harris uses DiCalcium Phosphate on his conures' food and provides mineral blocks at all times.

For a professional opinion on the need for calcium supplements and the use of grit, please consult your avian veterinarian. Also ask about egg binding as all the conure breeders interviewed cautioned to be on the alert for this problem during the laying season.

Note too that vitamin supplements used in conjunction with a vitamin rich pellet diet have proven to be toxic to birds, so use them only under the direction of your avian veterinarian.

*Conures and Company Aviary fresh fruit and vegetable mix for conures.*

## Diet

After much experimentation with different diets and supplements, Kam Pelham-Polk of Conures and Company Aviary now maintains all the conures at her breeding facility on the same diet. Her conures are fed a high quality medium-sized parrot pellet, a top quality parrot seed mix, and fresh fruits and vegetables every day. Her conures actually prefer their pellets mixed with the fruits and vegetables, which include various squash (whatever is in season), all types of peppers including hotter varieties (jalapenos, serranos etc.), apples, oranges, grapes, corncob, broccoli, kale, beets, sweet potatoes and other foods that look good or are in season. The soft food is chopped into chunks the size that conures can pick up with their feet and eat. The pellets and seed are mixed in the same dish, with the fresh fruits and vegetables placed on top. Fresh water is provided daily. At Saxe Point Aviary, Wendy and Bob Wilson create their soft food mix by chopping seasonal fruits and vegetables (such as pears, peaches, mango, banana, melon, zucchini and broccoli) into 12mm cubes and combining these with a base mix of apples, thawed frozen mixed vegetables, a seven bean mix and brown rice. The beans and rice are prepared by mixing together and cooking for five hours in a slow cooker. Unused portions are then frozen for storage.

Onto each portion being served, the Wilsons sprinkle a combination of parrot seed mix blended with small hookbill seed mix and topped with an almond or cracked walnut. This is offered in a separate food dish to the pellet dish. Pellets are always available to their birds.

At Rain Coast Aviary, the soft food mix is similar in content to that being fed at Saxe Point Aviary except that the large, parrot-sized good quality seed mixture (as well as a top quality pellet mix) is always available to the birds in a separate dish. The seed mix fed to their indoor birds contains no sunflower seed but that fed to their conures housed in outdoor flights does contain some sunflower seed. Soft foods include apples, oranges, mangos (when available), thawed mixed frozen vegetables and fruits and vegetables in season. Melons, especially cantaloupe, are relished by the birds. All items are chopped then mixed with cooked brown rice before serving. Each pair is fed a generous cup of this mix every day. Pairs with chicks receive two full dishes every day.

At Free Flyte Aviary, Judi Robben feeds all her conure species the same diet as her prized Painted Conures *Pyrrhura picta picta*. The parent birds are given conure size

pellets, which are available at all times. They are fed a variety of soft foods such as vegetables, fruits, beans, rice, pasta and sprouts every morning. Each bird gets one pistachio nut that has been cracked for them. The evening feed consists of 1/4 cup of seed per pair.

At Hill Country Aviaries in Texas, USA, Rick Jordan's pairs of Crimson-bellied Conures *Pyrrhura perlata perlata* receive a daily cup of sprouted sunflower seed, wheat, oats, millet, peas, carrot, apple, ZuPreem® Fruit Blend Breeder diet, soaked dried corn, fresh corn, and greens in the spring. ZuPreem® pellets contain corn meal, seed

*Bean mix for birds at Taylormade Aviary.*

meals, vitamins, minerals, fat, protein and amino acids providing balanced nutrition for parrots. For this reason Jordan does not need to supplement the birds' diet with calcium, vitamins or other additives.

James Taylor of Taylormade Aviaries, an avid and respected breeder of lories as well as conures, takes conure feeding a step further by introducing sprouted seed and lory nectar into his conures' soft food diet, the base of which is similar to those noted above. Seed sprouters are available from health food stores. The instructions must be followed carefully as sprouted seed can go off quickly on warm days and when not refrigerated.

All the conure keepers I interviewed feed additional soft food mix to their breeding pairs when chicks are being reared. At each of the aviary kitchens visited, large baskets of fresh fruit and vegetables were present. All keepers fed only top quality foods. Second best or bruised soft foods just will not do!

*Fresh fruit for birds at Taylormade Aviary.*

# ENTERTAINING CONURES

## Toys Really Are For Conures

Obviously, one way to satisfy any conure's appetite for investigation and destruction is to give it something to play with and chew. Conure toys can be purchased or be homemade. You may choose to dash down to your bird supply store for an armful of toys to satisfy even the most discriminating conure. However, if you know which materials are conure safe, any conure keeper will have fun dreaming up and constructing toys for their conure to investigate and chew to pieces.

Knowing what is safe to use when constructing a conure toy will also help the enthusiastic conure toy shopper to recognise a safe conure toy. When choosing (or making) a toy for your bird, always try to imagine the worst possible thing that could happen to an inquisitive conure. Will it get its head caught in that loop; will it chew off and swallow that bell clapper; will it get its toes caught in those tiny holes? No matter how safe a toy seems to be, it is wise to keep an eye on your pet's playtime with its toys. You should always do regular checks on the toys themselves: a damaged toy is a hazard to your conure.

*Sun Conures at 6 1/2 and 9 months of age in cage with toys.*

## Homemade Toys

Handmaking your conure toys need not be an expensive or complicated procedure. A little creativity, time and determination is all it takes.

Use only materials that are non-toxic to birds. There are no exceptions. For example, 100% cotton rope (undyed), willow or eucalyptus, stainless steel rope or chain are safe for birds. As a rule of thumb, if the materials are considered harmless for use when constructing children's toys, they should be safe when constructing a toy for your conure. But that is no guarantee. So, play it very safe.

Beware of hangers for toys that are noose-shaped, like shower curtain hooks. These can accidentally trap an unsuspecting conure during enthusiastic play. Under no circumstances should you use materials containing zinc or lead as these are toxic.

*Sun Conures at 6 1/2 and 9 months of age on a playgym.*

Even if they are plated with a non-toxic material such as plastic, the core is not safe from the strong bill of a conure. Here is an example of what a conure enthusiast used to construct her conure toys.

Sue Yakubowich did exhaustive research before creating her first conure toys for her companion pet bird *Oscar*, a Sharp-tailed Conure *Aratinga acuticaudata acuticaudata*. Yakubowich threaded various hard, large plastic beads (from a craft store) onto stainless steel wire (from a fishing supply store). For variation, she threaded non-toxic wood items such as wooden (pine) balls, by drilling a hole through the items and then threading them onto the stainless steel wire. These toys are hung in *Oscar's* cage or on the playgym with shoe strings (natural fibre shoe laces with the plastic ends

*Above: Example of a commercial conure playgym.*
*Below: Sharp-tailed Conure on a playgym.*

removed). *Oscar* also enjoys chewing wooden sticks (those used for frozen ice treats) and wooden clothes pegs, the old-fashioned kind without a metal spring. The pine balls, wooden sticks and wooden clothes pegs are available at craft and hobby shops.

## The Conure Playgym

On a playgym a conure not only exercises while at play, but also has the opportunity to mingle with its keeper. As such, the size and configuration of the playgym are determined by the available space to station it, and, of course, by the keeper's sense of aesthetics.

Commercial conure-sized playgyms are available at most bird supply stores, in all sorts of shapes and sizes, and for every budget. Some gyms are as simple as a single T-stand whereas others are so elaborate that they can fill a room. A wide range of playgyms are available between these two types.

As with conure toy construction, here too improvisation is an option. Devising and creating a playgym can be a lot of fun. A willow or eucalyptus branch (that has not been contaminated with chemicals such as insecticides) tucked into a Christmas tree stand,

J. ROBBEN

*Above: Painted Conures on a rope covered playgym.*
*Below: Conure chicks on a playgym.*

for example, positioned on top of a bed of yesterday's newspapers (to protect the floor), is an inexpensive option. (Wash and rinse the branches thoroughly before allowing your bird onto the gym – you never know what disease a wild bird may have deposited onto it.) A branch-in-a-stand type playgym is easily maintained by simply replacing the branch once soiled or chewed to pieces. Your conure will be kept amused stripping and gnawing the fresh branches. With the addition of a few toys to explore, the gym will be complete.

Please remember that it is irresponsible to leave a bird on its gym unsupervised. Yes, yes, yes, I can hear you arguing that your bird always stays put on its gym and that it has never attempted to fly off. However, pause and think of what might happen if it did... Conures are inquisitive creatures, with an innate need to inspect everything in their world! What would prevent your prized conure from wandering off and chewing on those poisonous plants you have been meaning to discard, or from gnawing through an electrical extension cord and electrocuting itself? Every home brims with potential bird hazards: stove tops, sharp utensils, open toilet bowls or other containers of water, and so on.

We hope you can see why supervision of your conure is so important, not just for your bird's safety but also for the good of your home furnishings. Conures are known for their destructive chewing ability – a sofa leg, a window sill, a wooden sculpture, a door frame, nothing could be more tempting for a beak-wielding conure with a propensity for trying everything.

PELHAM-POLK

# DISEASES AND DISORDERS COMMON TO CONURES

*Sharp-tailed Conure*

Although conures are a relatively hardy group of birds, they can develop illnesses or contract infections. Many of the problems avian veterinarians see in conures are similar to those seen in other parrots, and the reader is referred to Dr Michael J. Cannon's excellent book *A Guide to Basic Health and Disease in Birds*, ABK Publications for further information on these common illnesses, their cause and treatment. In this section I will discuss some of the problems which avian veterinarians regard as peculiar to conures and problems which present differently in conures compared to other parrots. I also want to discuss how you, as an aviculturist breeding conures or as a pet owner sharing your life with one, can assist in disease prevention.

When researching this section, I used the Internet to ask avian veterinarians around the world about diseases peculiar to conures. The response was overwhelming. I would like to take this opportunity to thank all those veterinarians both in Australia and overseas who so generously shared their thoughts with me. The Internet truly does make the world a smaller place!

## Hairworm or Threadworm (*Capillaria* species)

Avian veterinarians in Victoria, Australia have reported seeing drug-resistant *Capillaria* spp. (hairworm or threadworm) in conures. Undoubtedly the same situation occurs elsewhere. This worm lives in the proventriculus (stomach), ventriculus (gizzard) and intestine, causing enteritis and diarrhoea. Affected birds start to lose weight and look unwell. A faecal test is used to detect worm eggs in the droppings, however the worm is becoming more difficult to treat.

### Prevention and Treatment

Because this worm's lifecycle can be direct (birds eat the droppings of infected birds) or indirect (birds eat insects that have eaten the droppings of infected birds), prevention relies on good hygiene and preventing birds from having access to both droppings and insects. It is also essential that droppings are checked by a veterinarian before and after treatment to ensure that the worming preparation being used is effective.

If you suspect you have this problem in your birds, veterinary advice on treatment and control should be sought.

## Polyomavirus

Polyomavirus affects virtually all parrot species, and has also been reported in finches. The virus is shed in droppings, and other birds are infected when they inhale the dust from these droppings. Typically young chicks are the most susceptible, with most conure chick deaths occurring at less than six weeks of age, although it can occur later. Infected chicks may die suddenly, or have slow emptying crops, pale skin and bruising under the skin.

Survivors may appear normal or have abnormal feathering. Conure chicks that are older than six weeks of age when infected often do not show any signs of infection, but will shed the virus for a few months. Occasionally a bird will shed the virus for much longer – one veterinarian in the USA reported a bird shedding the virus for four years. These birds can obviously act as a source of infection to other birds. Most birds will eventually rid their body of the virus, but there have been reports of adult birds dying. Many of these birds had Circovirus (Psittacine Beak and Feather Disease) at the same time. This disease suppresses a bird's immunity to polyomavirus.

### Prevention and Treatment

As Budgerigars and lovebirds are commonly affected with polyomavirus, try to avoid keeping these birds if you have conures. If you do want to keep them, have them tested for polyomavirus.

Avoid buying conures aged less than 20 weeks. By then, the majority will have stopped shedding the virus if they had been exposed to it earlier. This does not remove the necessity for testing a new bird before introducing it to other birds.

In Australia, DNA testing is available for the detection of this virus. Overseas, a serological test for antibodies is also available. It would be advisable for anyone purchasing a conure to test for this disease before introducing the bird to their aviaries or other pets. Because of the nature of the DNA test, it is vital that the sample is collected by a veterinarian to prevent contamination, and that the results are carefully interpreted. Consult your avian veterinarian before undertaking any testing.

If you handrear birds, think twice about rearing someone else's chicks unless they or the parents have been tested (at least). Feed baby birds before going out to the aviaries to feed the adults. Do not come back in to the nursery without changing clothes and washing up. Any chicks that die should be autopsied to see if this disease is present in your collection.

In the USA, a vaccine is available, but it is not foolproof. It may help contain an outbreak, but it should not be relied on as a sole means of disease control or treatment.

## Conure Bleeding Syndrome

This bleeding disorder is fairly unique to conures. It was first reported in *Aratinga* species, and most reports since then have involved these larger conures.

Affected birds appear to cough up or sneeze blood (*epistaxis*), although some may bleed internally. Birds present acutely weak and lethargic, often with blood around the nares or beak. Blood tests often show that the bird is anaemic. Egg-laying hens are usually affected, and for this reason it is thought that it may be a calcium metabolism problem. Others suggest that it may be a virus or a bone marrow tumour.

*Epistaxis – a bleeding nose. This is an early sign of Conure Bleeding Syndrome.*

### Prevention and Treatment

Many veterinarians report that feeding a balanced pelleted diet, or supplementing the diet with calcium, can prevent this problem. Vitamin D3 injections will help with the absorption of dietary calcium.

Treatment is rest and warmth, with fluids or even blood transfusions to replace the lost blood. Calcium and Vitamin K appear to be of benefit and Vitamin D3 injections can help to absorb more calcium from the diet. Time is of the essence with these birds – if you see your bird showing these signs, see your veterinarian at once.

Conure Bleeding Syndrome remains a poorly understood condition at this time.

## Pacheco's Disease

This viral disease does not occur in Australia (yet). In most affected birds death occurs rapidly (in a matter of hours), with few clinical signs. (The occasional bird may have green urates, bloody diarrhoea and weakness before it dies, but even this is unusual.) Some birds infected with the virus do not show any clinical signs and then spread the disease within an aviary. Many conures, including the Patagonian, Sun, Nanday and Mitred Conure *Aratinga mitrata* have been implicated as asymptomatic carriers. Many avian veterinarians firmly believe that conures are frequent carriers. Therefore, it is an obvious consideration if importation of foreign birds is ever reinstated in Australia or when the origin of a bird elsewhere in the world is questionable.

The virus is shed in droppings and secretions from the eyes and nares, and birds are infected when they eat or inhale this infected material. The incubation period is 1–2 weeks, but in some cases can be longer. Outbreaks are often explosive, with birds dying throughout the aviary.

### Prevention and Treatment

There is no reliable, foolproof way of detecting carrier birds, although both blood tests and DNA tests are available in the USA. Vaccination is also available in the USA but, as with the polyomavirus vaccine, it should not be relied on as a sole means of disease control. Birds exposed to an outbreak, but not yet sick, can be treated with acyclovir.

## Proventricular Dilatation Disease

This is (probably) a viral disease seen in nearly all parrot species overseas, including conures. Fortunately, only one suspect case has been seen in Australia (in a macaw), and good quarantine procedures by the bird's owner stopped this disease from spreading.

Although classically only the proventriculus is affected, other organs such as the adrenal glands and the brain have also been affected. Typically, infected birds are hungry, lose weight, regurgitate their food and may have undigested food in their droppings. They may become quiet and depressed, or show neurological signs if the brain is affected. Death inevitably results.

### Prevention and Treatment

At this time there are no reliable tests in the live bird that can be used for routine screening, nor is there any vaccination. Incubation periods for the disease can be quite long, so quarantine may not prevent its spread.

If and when importation is re-opened in Australia, people thinking of importing birds should only buy birds from reliable sources, known to be free of the disease, and watch new birds closely for any signs of illness.

## Egg Binding

*Aratinga* conures, in particular, seem to be affected by egg binding. This occurs when an egg is not passed from the hen in the normal amount of time and the hen is unable to expel it. There are many possible causes, including calcium deficiency, obesity, poor nutrition, cold weather and uterine infections.

'Penguin Pose' - the typical posture of an egg-bound Sun Conure hen.

Calcium deficiencies and obesity seem to be the most common factors in hens that are egg-bound.

Affected birds are fluffed up, sit right back on their tails and waddle when walking (the 'Penguin' look). They sometimes have difficulty breathing, and will bob their tails and open their mouths when breathing. The egg can often (but not always) be felt in the abdomen.

*Post-mortem photograph of an egg-bound bird. Note the egg still in the oviduct and a fresh follicle developing.*

### Prevention and Treatment

Prevention is primarily based on diet and exercise. Keeping your bird lean and fit, and giving her plenty of calcium, is vital. Pet birds should not be encouraged to lay eggs. This can be achieved by keeping them on a low fat and low sugar diet. A diet of maintenance pellets and vegetables can achieve this, while keeping them in excellent health.

If a pet hen does start laying eggs, it is best to leave them with her (when she lays a normal clutch size she will often stop), reduce the amount of daylight (this tricks her into thinking it is winter) and move her cage to another room (this stresses her a little, just enough to take her mind off sex!). If this fails, hormone therapy and/or surgery can usually solve the problem.

Treatment depends on how stressed the hen is looking. If she seems uncomfortable, but not stressed, putting her in a warm hospital cage and giving her some calcium syrup (eg Calcivet™) may be sufficient. If, however, she shows signs of distress, for example if she is unable to stand, is gasping for air or is fluffed up, consult your veterinarian immediately. Some of these birds will need to have the egg collapsed internally to save their lives. This procedure should be left to an expert.

## Megabacteria

This problem was first noted in Budgerigars and has since spread to many other bird species, including nearly all parrots, finches and even ostriches. It has been seen in conures both in Australia and overseas.

Recent research in the USA indicates that this is actually a fungal infection. The fungus lines the proventriculus (stomach), causing ulcerations and poor digestion of food. Affected birds are ravenously hungry, but continue to lose weight. Undigested seed and food can be seen in the droppings.

The infection is spread when a bird eats the droppings of an infected bird. The conures that I have seen with megabacteria were housed with other species of parrots in aviaries with dirt floors.

### Treatment

Diagnosis can only be made by the detection of the megabacteria in faecal samples. Treatment is with amphotericin B. Consult your veterinarian for an accurate diagnosis and correct treatment regime.

# Heavy Metal Poisoning

Because of their love of chewing, conures can be very prone to heavy metal (lead and zinc) poisoning. Although frequently associated with poor quality aviary wire, lead and zinc are very common in our environment. Lead is stored in the body, and so frequent exposure to small amounts will eventually lead to poisoning. Zinc, on the other hand, is not stored, and so poisoning requires exposure to toxic levels of zinc in a short period.

Typically, affected birds are fluffed up, lethargic and have stopped eating. They may drink large amounts of water and produce very watery droppings. Regurgitation and vomiting are very common, and the crop can often be felt to be full of water. Occasionally blood will be passed with the droppings. Lead often causes fitting and convulsions, and may be associated with feather picking and foot chewing.

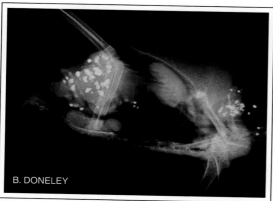

B. DONELEY

*X-Ray of a bird with heavy metal poisoning. The bright white spots are metal in the crop, gizzard and proventriculus.*

## Treatment

Diagnosis is based on a history of exposure to lead or zinc, recognition of the clinical signs, X-rays to assess the condition of the bird's internal organs and to determine if metal particles are in the gizzard. Blood tests may be necessary to measure the lead levels in the bird's body.

Fortunately, if the owner picks up the early signs of illness, treatment is usually successful. It consists of injections of a drug that chelates (binds) lead or zinc, allowing its excretion from the body. At the same time, treatment is given to remove any unabsorbed metal from the gizzard. Many of these birds also have internal organ damage, especially to the kidneys and the pancreas. This will also require treatment. Heavy metal poisoning is not something that can be readily treated at home, at least not until the bird is stabilised.

# Footnote - Noise

Even though this has been discussed earlier in this book, it is worth mentioning again. Alex Rosenwax, a Sydney avian veterinarian has reported that conures are the most common pet birds that he is asked to find new homes for. The reason for this is that the owners cannot cope with the noise. Conures can be incredibly noisy, and I think that all aviculturists and pet owners need to be aware of this and work on the problem before it gets out of hand.

Breeders should ensure that people purchasing pet conures are aware of just how noisy they can be. Remember that this is not abnormal behaviour on the bird's part, but is, in fact, normal behaviour expressed inappropriately.

## Prevention

Excessive noise may be prevented by trying some of the strategies and suggestions outlined in this book. However, do not be afraid to seek further professional advice from an avian veterinarian or a qualified animal behaviourist.

# PREVENTION OF DISEASE

Although bird owners are getting better at recognising signs of illness and avian veterinarians have access to better and improved diagnostic tests and treatments, it is still more sensible (and cheaper!) to prevent disease rather than treat it. While we will never have a husbandry system that guarantees no disease ever, we can implement management changes that will reduce the chances of disease outbreaks.

This sort of prevention management revolves around two key principles:

a) preventing disease entering your aviary or home in the first place; and

b) minimising the spread and impact of disease if it does appear.

## Preventing the Entry of Disease

This is surprisingly easier than it sounds. There are three key steps:

1. Only obtain birds from a reliable source.
2. Quarantine birds before allowing them entrance.
3. Test and treat for common or significant diseases.

If you are considering purchasing a conure, ask around for reliable outlets (as discussed earlier in this book). If possible, inspect the aviary or pet shop and talk to the aviculturist or shop owner. Look for some guarantee of quality and care, eg MAP registration or equivalent. Do not buy from the first place you visit – shop around and compare. Remember, good quality birds are rarely cheap. If you are not satisfied with the standard of care and hygiene, do not buy birds from that breeder or shop.

Quarantine serves two purposes. Firstly, it helps to keep disease out. Many diseases have an incubation period of less than six weeks, and will therefore reveal themselves during the quarantine period. Parasitic diseases (worms, lice and coccidiosis) can also be eliminated during the quarantine period so that the new bird does not introduce them to your other birds. Quarantine also allows your bird a step-by-step introduction to a new life. Instead of having to deal with new bird companions, a new owner, unfamiliar surroundings and a change in diet, at the one time quarantine allows all of these to be phased in gradually, so that the final introduction to the home or aviary is not as traumatic.

Place your new bird in an area of the yard or the house where it does not share the same air space as the other birds. Feed it after the other birds, using the same type of food and dishes that your other birds access. This accustoms the bird to you and your management, and at the same time prevents your tracking disease from the new bird to the others. Keep a close eye on your new acquisition, and seek veterinary advice if something does not look right. New birds should remain in quarantine for a minimum of six weeks.

There are some diseases that may not show up in the quarantine period (eg polyomavirus and worms). For this reason, you should work with your avian veterinarian to develop a testing program for new birds. You should test for problems that are realistically going to affect you, and for which tests are available. I would recommend that Australian bird owners test new conures for worms, lice, polyomavirus and chlamydia as a minimum. However, testing for Pacheco's Disease would not be warranted in Australia (at the moment) but may be advisable in other countries. Consult your avian veterinarian to develop a list of problems and diseases that should be tested for in your area. If you do find a problem, it is better to treat (or cull) the one bird in quarantine than to risk your entire collection.

## Minimising the Spread and Impact of Disease

Even the best quarantine systems can go wrong. Disease can be spread so easily –

via the air, on your hands, clothing and shoes, on water and feed dishes, and so on. Therefore, you need to have a second line of defence to fall back on if something does go wrong.

Minimising the spread and impact of disease has two key elements:
- how you manage the birds; and
- the birds themselves.

You need to assess what you consider to be the most important feature of your collection. For most breeders, it will be their breeding birds. For pet owners, it may be their favourite bird. Whichever you choose, that becomes sacrosanct – it must be protected at all costs. It should be the first area attended to each day. Nothing should be permitted into that area without being quarantined and tested. You must plan your day's work so that you are not continually tracking through that area. If possible, design the layout of your aviaries so that you do not backtrack from one area to another. You may need to delegate certain tasks, for example the person who looks after the adult birds doesn't go near the nurseries, and vice versa. Look at how disease can be spread, and plan to prevent it.

The impact of disease is greatly influenced by the health of the birds themselves. What might normally be a minor illness in healthy, well-fed birds could be a disaster in stressed, malnourished birds. Birds can endure a lot, but there is a breaking point! A good diet and annual health checks should be an integral part of your management.

I will not go into great detail on what constitutes a good diet, which has already been covered in this title, other than to say it is not just seed!

Conures are fun, entertaining and rewarding birds to take into your life. Good management and careful planning means a healthy bird, that does what you want it to do – to breed well, or to be a companion. Be aware of the possible health problems but, more importantly, be aware of how to prevent them.

## Diseases Diagnosed in 140 Conures

| | |
|---|---|
| Polyomavirus | 29 (20.7%) |
| Bacterial Infection | 28 (20%) |
| Proventricular Dilatation Disease | 21 (15%) |
| Nutritional Problems | 15 (10.7%) |
| Cancer | 13 (9.3%) |
| Pacheco's Disease | 10 (7.1%) |
| Allergic Dermatitis | 10 (7.1%) |
| Fungal Respiratory Disease | 7 (5%) |
| Chlamydia | 3 (2.1%) |
| Circovirus | 2 (1.4%) |
| Adenovirus | 2 (1.4%) |

*(Information provided by Dr Robert Schmidt DVM, avian and exotic veterinary pathologist, California, USA.)*

# SPECIES

Pair of
Crimson-bellied
Conures

P ODEKERKEN

# CONURE TAXONOMY

This seems a good place to pause, catch our breath and take a few moments for an introduction to taxonomy – the classification of living (and extinct) organisms – and for a word on how taxonomy relates to our discussion of conures.

Avian taxonomists have divided conure parrots into several separate groups called genus, species and subspecies.

Genus describes a group whose members have similar characteristics, that also make them distinct from other organisms. This book discusses five genus of conures: *Nandayus, Guaruba, Cyanoliseus, Aratinga* and *Pyrrhura*.

*'Sunday' and Nanday (right) Conures. The 'Sunday' is a hybrid of the Sun and Janday Conures.*

A species describes a group or groups within the genus that not only have common characteristics but that are also capable of interbreeding. Using the Crimson-bellied Conure *Pyrrhura perlata perlata* as an example, it is a member of the genus *Pyrrhura* and is of the species *perlata*.

A subspecies is a group that is very similar to the group or groups within a species but has a slight variance (say, in colour) which often relates to its geographic isolation from the rest of the group or groups. Continuing with the *Pyrrhura perlata perlata* example, it is a member of the genus *Pyrrhura*, is within the species *perlata*, and is the nominate form of the subspecies *perlata*.

A hybrid can occur should members from different genus, species or subspecies interbreed. For example, should the Sun Conure *Aratinga solstitialis* breed with the Janday Conure *Aratinga jandaya*, they would produce the hybrid 'Sunday' Conure. (Hybrids rarely occur in the wild and thus are frowned upon in aviculture because of the mixing of pure bloodlines.)

## A Simple Method for Conure Genus Identification

Here is a simplified method for identifying a conure genus at a glance.

*Nandayus* is the only debatable genus. You will either have to familiarise yourself with the appearance of its sole member, the Nanday Conure *Nandayus nenday*, or agree with Rosemary Low who argues that it has little in anatomical difference to justify classifying it in its own genus, and thus believes that it should fall under the *Aratinga* genus. Visually, it is easily identifiable. The Nanday Conure *Nandayas nenday* has a black mask and red socks, a combination which is very distinctive.

Genus *Guaruba* is also identifiable by its single member, the Queen of Bavaria's Conure *Guaruba guarouba*. There is no mistaking this genus! It is a brilliant yellow conure with dark green wing tips and a majestic beak. Interestingly, the genus *Guaruba* recently sprang from the ranks of *Aratinga*.

The genus *Cyanoliseus* also has but one species as a member, the Patagonian Conure

*The Nanday Conure, genus Nandayus is easily identifiable by its black mask and red socks.*

*Left: Queen of Bavaria's Conure Guaruba guarouba, the single member of the genus.*
*Below right: Patagonian Conure genus Cyanoliseus.*

*Cyanoliseus patagonus,* but has three subspecies: the Lesser Patagonian Conure *Cyanoliseus patagonus patagonus,* the Greater Patagonian Conure *Cyanoliseus patagonus byroni* and the Andean Patagonian Conure *Cyanoliseus patagonus andinus.* To identify this genus, just look for the uniquely feathered cere.

All members of the genus *Pyrrhura* display a scalloped bib, unique to this group.

Through the process of elimination regarding the genus covered in this book, the remaining conures belong to the genus *Aratinga.*

## The *Aratinga*-Versus-*Pyrrhura* Debate

An ongoing debate in species preference is the selection of *Aratinga* over *Pyrrhura* members. Each genus has features which vary in degrees of attractiveness.

Rosemary Low recommends *Aratingas* as aviary birds despite their reputation for being destructive and noisy. In their favour she cites their friendliness, liveliness and entertainment value. Low ranks the larger *Aratingas* comparable in intelligence to the small macaws, adding that 'some species nest readily and prove prolific in captivity.' The bird is friendly, lively, entertaining, intelligent, easy to breed. What more could one want of a conure?

The *Pyrrhura* is arguably less destructive, quieter and much more loving than the *Aratinga.*

Low said it best while singing the praises of *Pyrrhura,* saying that they have an endearing personality, are 'steady, if not tame,' are highly inquisitive and are willing breeders (often extremely prolific). All are easy to care for and can be highly recommended to the beginner and the experienced aviculturist alike.

*Above left: Golden-crowned Conure Aratinga aurea.*

*Right: Maroon-bellied Conure Pyrrhura frontalis.*
*Note the scalloped bib.*

# COLOUR MUTATIONS IN CONURE SPECIES

Due to the increasing popularity of conure species as captive birds, colour mutation have started to appear. With time we can expect the appearance of all the same colou that occur in other domesticated parrot species such as Budgerigars, lovebirds, India Ringnecked Parrots and other species.

The naming of these mutations should follow the rules established for other specie However, as many of these colours are new, there has been limited opportunity to ful explore the genetic nature of these mutations and their outcomes when these are teste against other colour mutations still to be discovered and established. Hence we cann be certain that many of the names given to these colours are correct.

Blue mutations are generally easy to identify, but in some instances Parblu (Turquoise) mutations can be difficult to distinguish until combined with Lutino to produc a Creamino if they are Parblue mutations, or an Albino if they are 'true' Blue mutation

The 'Yellow-sided' mutation in Green-cheeked Conures seems unusual and current defies assignment to an established mutational form. However, once more examples similar sex-linked mutations are established in other conures, we may decide that this not so unusual. This mutation may simply be the South American parrot version of th Opaline mutation.

The greatest area of debate involves the naming of so-called 'Cinnamon' mutation Many are not true 'Cinnamon' mutations, which must be sex-linked and preve conversion of brown melanin into black melanin. These presumed 'Cinnamo mutations may eventually be identified as other albinistic mutations such Fallow, Faded and Par-ino (Lime). At this point in time it is best to view the simply as melanin altering mutations which are still to be correctly identifie

## Known Colour Mutations in Conures
### Dusky-headed Conure
- Blue
### Golden-crowned Conure
- Blue • Cinnamon (see discussion above)
### Green-cheeked Conure
- Blue • Cinnamon (see discussion above)
- Parblue (Turquoise - see discussion above)
- Yellow-sided (see discussion above)
### Maroon-bellied Conure
- Cinnamon (see discussion above) • Lutino
### Nanday Conure
- Cinnamon (see discussion above) • Lutino
### Painted Conure
- Pied
### Sharp-tailed Conure
- Blue • Lutino
### Sun Conure
- Lutino • Pied

*Above left: Cinnamon Nanday Conure.*
*Centre left: Cinnamon Green-cheeked Conure.*
*Bottom left: Normal (left) and Yellow-sided Green-cheeked Conures.*
*Above right: Pied Sun Conure chick.*
*Centre right: Cinnamon Yellow-sided Green-cheeked Conure.*
*Bottom right: Parblue Green-cheeked Conure.*

# OVERTURE TO SPECIES SPECIFICS

In this section of the book, we will look at each of the popular conures in detail. Note: not all conure species are included here. Many other species exist and are gaining in popularity in aviculture. This book focuses on the popular conures being kept in aviculture worldwide.

Each species will be discussed under the following headings:

## Terminology

We took a few wrong turns, even venturing up some blind alleys and dead ends, while researching the species discussed in this book. The common names proved confusing and often ambiguous. For instance, we found that what is commonly referred to as a 'Blue-crowned Conure' is actually a Sharp-tailed Conure *Aratinga acuticaudata acuticaudata*. In the end, it was the scientific name that saved the day ie Sharp-tailed Conure is *Aratinga acuticaudata acuticaudata* whereas the Blue-crowned Conure is *A. acuticaudata haemorrhus,* another subspecies.

It is a good idea to learn and use the scientific names, because the common names can prove misleading. For example, the common name 'Golden-crowned' can apply to many different species of birds. Then there are language barriers to consider. For example, *Aratinga weddellii* is most often called the Dusky-headed Conure in English, but is called the *Braunkopfsittich* in German which translates as Brown-headed Parrakeet! Therefore, if we all become used to calling a bird by its scientific name, we can eliminate confusion as the scientific name remains the same for every language. For this reason I have generally referred to the conures using their scientific name. In this way, we can all become accustomed to seeing and using the correct terminology.

The pronunciation of scientific names should pose few problems. Generally the names are pronounced as they look. Simply pronounce each syllable slowly. Now try saying *Aratinga* out loud. It is easy! *Aratinga*, by the way, means 'little macaw'. As a matter of interest the word conure is derived from the Greek *konos* cone + *ourás* tail.

## Introduction and Pet Quality

This section looks at why you should consider keeping this species: its qualities as a pet and as an aviary bird and its drawbacks, if any. Included are the individual experiences of seasoned owners and experienced breeders.

## Description

To assist in the area of identification of each conure (and to ensure that the bird is not a hybrid), an accurate physical description has been supplied by renowned and highly respected aviculturist Rosemary Low. Our own observations are added for good measure.

## In the Wild

Bird keepers always wonder what their bird's life would have been like, living in the wild: where it would live, what it would feed on, how it would behave in its flock. Knowing something of a conure's native habitat arms the conscientious keeper with an idea of what kind of environment to create for the captive birds to most approximate a natural home – whether by providing foliage for the secretive canopy dweller, or ample flying room for the savannah dweller, for instance. Likewise, knowing the conure's choice of housing and diet in the wild assists in fulfilling its needs in captivity.

Knowing how the individuals of the species behave in the wild also offers insight into the species' behaviour in captivity. Some conures, for example, are very shy or secretive animals in the wild, which may explain why they behave that way in captivity. At the other end of the spectrum, some species are so gregarious that they make themselves quite at home in human settlement, even making a nuisance of themselves. One could conclude that those species would easily make themselves quite at home in the residence or aviary of their keeper.

Quite by coincidence, all the conures in this book inhabit areas within South America. (Other conure species are native to Central America, Mexico and the Caribbean.) Join us as we travel, albeit in our imagination, to the lush, tropical rainforests and semi-arid savannahs of South America, for sightings of indigenous conure parrots. Some will be quite common and be everywhere, while others will be almost invisible, blending with foliage in the forest canopy. Sadly, some will be absent from view because of their very few numbers.

As expected, we will see that human encroachment into conure habitat is the main reason for the decline of those conures. Others, however, seem to have adapted well to human habitation, even increasing their numbers. Here, humans are unwitting providers of the wild conure diet, of seeds (agricultural crops) and fruits (orchards).

We will discover that little, if any, interaction occurs between different conure species, with each claiming its own territory. Equally astonishing, we will find that very little has been recorded about wild conures, even those that are very commonly seen. Wild conure study is in its infancy.

Nevertheless, come along as we view conures in a wide range of habitats. Some inhabit savannahs and dry lands, others are only seen high up in the rainforest canopy, yet others favour the bush along river banks. Some conures too, are found high in the mountains where nights can be quite chilly.

## Breeding

Some of the conures discussed in this book are not only on the brink of extinction in the wild, but are also extremely rare in aviculture. Those conures are therefore dependent on captive breeding to ensure that they do not become extinct. It is understood that those species will have to be bred in sufficiently large numbers before they can even be considered for the pet trade.

However, the more common species also require our help. Their growing popularity is creating a large demand for birds for the pet trade.

Some of the conures in this book have proven to be prolific breeders in captivity, while others can be tricky and thus require experience, dedication and a lot of patience. When breeding, some of the conures favour tree trunks, others a natural cave, or even a nestbox hung sideways. Even the configuration of the nestbox or variety of configurations you may need to offer may surprise you.

Here too you will find a species or two that may fit into your goal to establish a mixed aviary or a communal breeding facility.

Within the discussion that follows, you will discover differences of opinion regarding down colour on some species. Judi Robben explains that 'if you do not see the chick the day it hatches or shortly thereafter, you might miss their hatching down.' And Rick Jordan further explains: 'Usually when an aviculturist says down colour changes to grey, they are seeing the emergence of new feather growth at the skin level and it makes the white down look that way. Actually most chicks begin to lose the down when feathers begin to form under the skin.'

Join us as we learn, from successful breeders, some of the methods they use to breed even the rarest of conure species.

P ODEKERKEN

# SHARP-TAILED CONURE
## *Aratinga acuticaudata acuticaudata*

### Terminology

The Sharp-tailed Conure *A. a. acuticaudata* has been incorrectly named the Blue-crowned Conure which is another subspecies *A. a. haemorrhous* as Kremer quotes. Arndt, on the other hand, labels the nominate form of the species and the three subspecies as Blue-crowned Conures (rather than as members of the Sharp-tailed family).

Low blames the nomenclature confusion on the aviculturists who generalise, using the term 'Blue-crowned' when referring to the nominate form of the species, the Sharp-tailed Conure. She points out that the subspecies *A. a. haemorrhous* is a truly rare bird in aviculture, whereas Sharp-tailed Conures were exported in great numbers from Argentina, Bolivia, and Paraguay during the 1980s.

Therefore, the commonly available conure known generally as the Blue-crowned Conure, is actually the Sharp-tailed Conure. I suggest we begin calling these birds by their correct name, the Sharp-tailed Conure, or better, the Acuticaudata Conure or best, *A. a. acuticaudata*. *Acuticaudata* means 'sharp-tailed'.

### Introduction and Pet Quality

Michael Lockey, Director of Evergreen Acres Bird Sanctuary regards the Sharp-tailed Conure as the highest form of avian life, bar none. Lockey is so ecstatic about this species that he feels that they have the potential to become as popular as Budgerigars and cockatiels. He offers many reasons for this belief: their intelligence, their talking ability (albeit limited to a few words or phrases), their relaxed manner (they are not easily stressed) and their very affectionate nature. Rosemary Low, in fact, deems them to be the most intelligent of all the conure species. But Low hastens to warn of their potential for raucous cacophony, citing their loud voices as their main drawback.

Thomas Arndt defends the Sharp-tailed Conure saying that this so-called loud noise should be forgiven in exchange for the entertainment they provide. However, being forgiving does not make them any quieter! Arndt, therefore cautions that although they only rarely use their piercing voices, the neighbours should be considered when contemplating this conure for an outdoor aviary.

*A Sharp-tailed Conure at ease with its keeper.*

Arndt commends the Sharp-tailed Conure for being equally well-suited to all levels of bird keeping, from the novice conure keeper through to the experienced. Nevertheless, you should expect some stress while the bird settles down and becomes accustomed to its new surroundings. Evidently it is worth the wait. Except in very large aviaries, these birds will usually tame down. Single birds, of course, become tame more quickly.

Arndt has determined them to be cold hardy, providing of course, that they have been acclimatised and have access to a heated room when winter temperatures dip

*A Sharp-tailed Conure snuggling.*

more than a few degrees below freezing.

Kam Pelham-Polk, who maintains 25 proven breeding pairs of Sharp-tailed Conures, is absolutely enamoured with them. 'Of the larger conures they make one of the best pets available.' Pelham-Polk has found them to be gentle birds, that do not tend to nip unless antagonised.

Nevertheless, Pelham-Polk finds that these conures like to have the last word and they do this by what she refers to as 'grumbling'. She believes that domestically bred Sharp-tailed Conures will remain tame without daily handling. She goes so far as to say that they can go several weeks without physical interaction with their keepers. When one of these conures has been cage bound for an unusually long time and is finally taken out, 'it may grumble at having been neglected but it will be just as sweet and tame as it ever was.' Evidently, they are very forgiving!

Pelham-Polk is enthusiastic about their talking ability. 'I have always told my baby bird buyers that the talking ability of a Sharp-tailed Conure is limited only by what they want to teach their particular bird. As a rule, the voice is very clear and easily understood, not garbled or harsh.'

Like Arndt, Pelham-Polk points to the entertainment value of this species. She likens them to clowns – as they like to chew, climb and swing from the top of their cage by a single toe, enjoying a plentiful supply of toys.

## Description

Low describes the Sharp-tailed Conure thus: 'Recognised by its dull blue head, in some birds the breast is also tinged with blue. The rest of the plumage is green, except the tail feathers which are brownish red at the base of the inner webs and the underwing coverts which are olive-yellow. The upper mandible is horn-coloured with a dark tip and the lower mandible is blackish. The iris is orange-red and there is an area of bare white skin surrounding the eye.' The length is 36cm and weight approximately 155–170 grams.

*A Sharp-tailed Conure.*

Compared to other conures, the Sharp-tailed Conure is not one of the smaller examples.

## In the Wild

The Sharp-tailed Conure is a good example of a commonly seen bird with little known about its wild behaviour. These conures inhabit an area covering southern Brazil, northern Argentina, Paraguay and Uruguay in South America. Common and frequently seen in their normal range of the drier regions, they have adapted to all but the humid woodland regions. Rather than keeping to the forest canopy, these conures prefer the lowland scrub bushes and open savannah. Kremer says that they travel in flocks outside of the breeding season. During breeding season, like most of the conures described in this book, they prefer their privacy and retreat from the flock to nest, usually in a tree cavity, as high up as seven metres.

Arndt adds to this knowledge saying that this species is nomadic and shows little shyness when in the open. Their diet includes fruits, cactus, some seeds and the blossoms of the ciebo tree.

Although Sharp-tailed Conures can wreak havoc on grain fields, Kremer defends them, arguing that since their appetite for cultivated grains includes a taste for weed seeds, they do some good too!

## Breeding

Arndt urges separating these conures into individual pairs, especially during the breeding season. Like most *Aratinga* members, they become aggressive towards other birds, including their own kind, at this time. He recommends housing them in an aviary measuring 3 metres long x 1 metre wide x 2 metres high with a roomy tree hollow or spacious nestbox.

Kremer advises that standard cockatiel nestboxes work well. He also speaks of successes with boxes measuring 30cm square x 45cm high but recommends one measuring 50–60cm in height and 15–20cm square with an entrance hole 8cm in diameter. A thick layer of non-toxic wood shavings is suitable to line the box.

Once the roost is accepted, the birds are ready to breed. Arndt recommends positioning the nestbox horizontally so that the eggs will not be trampled underfoot. The hen lays one clutch of three eggs per year with a complete hatchout. (However, Pelham-Polk's hens may lay up to three clutches per year with complete hatchout).

Unlike Arndt, Pelham-Polk has not seen aggression in her birds, whether they are in breeding mode or not. That is not to say that they do not become aggressive toward their keeper when they are nesting. The cock, in particular, will become extremely protective of his mate and the nest.

Pelham-Polk has set up her breeding facility so that all of her pairs are able to see and hear each other. She has found that each pair does best in a 95cm square x 122cm long cage or flight, which gives them plenty of room to exercise and move around.

With regard to the nestbox, Pelham-Polk's ideas are actually the opposite of Arndt's (who suggests a roomy box). She explains that a problem with breeding the Sharp-tailed Conure is the size of the nestbox. These conures like the security of a smaller nestbox. She uses a nestbox measuring 25cm square x 25cm high and has had great success. The depth of the box can vary according to the pair's needs but the other dimensions should always be 25cm x 25cm. There is plenty of room for the conure pair to get into the box and sit on the eggs. Many breeders have expressed concern about the length of the tail. However this does not pose a problem as the tail will bend to fit the box. All of her pairs of Sharp-tailed Conures sleep in their nestboxes at night whether they are breeding or not. She has tried metal nestboxes but has found that the conures prefer timber boxes.

Pelham-Polk's pairs usually lay 2–4 eggs, with the average clutch consisting of three eggs which are all fertile. Although her pairs may lay up to three clutches a year, she has never had to remove a nestbox to dissuade them from breeding, as the birds tend to take a break on their own. She also mentions that nesting pairs make good foster parents. Pelham-Polk pulls the chicks at 2–2 1/2 weeks of age.

She makes sure that all of her birds have plenty of toys to play with and to chew. This helps distract the birds from demolishing their nestbox. 'Although I have not found them to be overly destructive,' explains Pelham-Polk, 'Sharp-tailed Conures love to chew!'

Robben reports that her Sharp-tailed Conures incubate for about 23 days, the chicks hatch with white down, and fledge between 7–8 weeks of age.

**GOLDEN-CROWNED CONURE**
*Aratinga aurea aurea*

P ODEKERKEN

# GOLDEN-CROWNED CONURE
*Aratinga aurea aurea*

## Terminology

The Golden-crowned Conure *A. a. aurea* is also commonly known as the Peach-fronted Conure.

Reference texts advise not to confuse the Golden-crowned Conure with the Petz's or Half-moon Conure *Aratinga canicularis canicularis* which, most noticeably, has a horn-coloured beak. The Golden-crowned Conure has a black beak. *Aurea* means 'golden' in Latin.

## Introduction and Pet Quality

Golden-crowned Conures have been a favourite of conure keepers for over a century. Thomas Arndt suggests that they make good pet birds as they are relatively quiet, are capable of becoming tame, have an ability to mimic some human sounds and whistles and are intelligent birds. Understandably, with all these qualities in their favour, it is no wonder that this conure is so popular.

However, do not lose sight that these are conures and, like most conures, they can be destructive and noisy. To pacify their need to gnaw, they should be kept supplied with fresh twigs.

As for their loudness, like other tame conures, the Golden-crowned Conure can be vociferous, mainly when disturbed or while performing their morning greetings and evening pre-roosting rituals.

In the aviary, Arndt describes this species as being cautious but not shy, and safe to house communally with smaller birds except during the breeding season. He suggests using a flight as small as 2.5 metres long x 1 metre wide x 2 metres high as

*Golden-crowned Conure on top of a once painted cage.*

these birds are, in his estimation, not very demanding. Because of their reputation as avid gnawers, he cautions about the use of unprotected timber in an aviary. He adds that these conures are hardy once acclimatised.

Kremer differs with Arndt's assessment on how undemanding the Golden-crowned Conure is in its need for living space. Kremer claims that they are strong flyers and suggests that they appreciate a long flight. He too, however, warns of their piercing voice but does qualify this by saying that after they become accustomed to their new accommodation, they will limit their vocals mainly to morning and evening calls. Like many of the *Aratinga* genus, these conures enjoy bathing.

Judi Robben believes that they make good pets. She feels that they can be affectionate and endearing, that they are beautiful, and that they have a talent for mimicry. They are less noisy than the larger *Aratinga* members although a bit noisier than the *Pyrrhuras*. Because she also raises Painted Conures *P. p. picta*, many of Robben's observations compare the two genus. For instance, when it comes to vocals, Robben explains: 'These conures are a bit louder and shriller in their calls than Painted

Conures. They have a clearer voice when they imitate human speech. They are very intelligent birds and can be taught to repeat a few words, imitate sounds and even whistle short melodies.' Robben adds that every bird is an individual, so some are quicker to mimic than others. 'As pets, they are not known to be loud even though they belong to the *Aratinga* family.'

Robben does believe that this species should be handled on a daily basis to keep them from becoming nippy and to keep them 'sweet and mellow.' Since they love to chew, Robben stresses that since they can be destructive (although less so than the Sun Conure *A. solstitialis* and the Janday Conure *A. jandaya*), they should be provided with a good supply of timber and leather toys to keep them occupied and happy.

Robben states that unlike many other conure species that like to roost in their nestbox year round, they usually sleep on perches (except when they are breeding).

*Golden-crowned Conure.*

## Description

At a glance, the Golden-crowned Conure is a green bird with an orange forehead and blue crown accentuated by a black beak. An unusual feature is the golden orange feathers surrounding its eyes (not a naked eye ring). Some birds have only a few or none of these brightly coloured eye ring feathers. Often, as Arndt adamantly states, these are immature birds.

Low describes the Golden-crowned Conure thus: 'The forehead, part of the crown and a narrow ring of feathers surrounding the eye are orange. Hindcrown is blue and the cheeks and throat are olive-green. Primaries are bluish, tipped with black. The rest of the plumage is dark green above and light green below, tending to yellowish olive on the breast and underside of the tail. The tail is green, tipped with blue. The bill is black and the iris is brown'. The length is 26cm and the weight approximately 70–80 grams.

## In the Wild

Golden-crowned Conures are common birds over almost all of their enormous range. They live in trees and bushes of the savannahs north of Argentina, throughout Brazil (except for the coastal areas and the south-east), the eastern half of Bolivia and the northern half of Paraguay in South America. They also range south into the northern tip of Argentina but are not commonly seen there. With such a vast territory, the Golden-crowned Conure has one of the widest distribution of all *Aratinga* conures.

Their prolific numbers within such a huge territory may be an indication of this species' ability to adapt. Kremer, in fact, speculates that even with human encroachment and the inevitable destruction of the rainforests, this conure may be on the increase and becoming even more widespread. These conures are often observed close to human habitation so it is not surprising when Kremer says that they are not very shy and that they take little notice of human activity while foraging. The birds travel in individual pairs or in groups of between 10 and 30, and occasionally more, individuals.

Arndt agrees that the Golden-crowned Conure lacks shyness and adds that they become so intent on foraging that they are not easily disturbed. His observations are that they forage for the greater part of the day on seeds, nuts, berries, fruits, insects and larvae. As these birds are so common, it is surprising when Arndt states that almost nothing is known of their natural breeding behaviour except that they nest in tree cavities and knotholes. Kremer adds that, in the wild, a clutch usually consists of 2–4 eggs.

## Breeding

For Arndt, the Golden-crowned Conure, along with the Sun Conure A. *solstitialis* and the Janday Conure A. *jandaya*, are among the most easily bred of the *Aratinga* family. His main caution is to be sure that the nestbox is sufficiently insulated to keep the eggs from becoming chilled because egg laying can begin in late winter. He notes that two clutches are possible with a third even probable, and that each clutch consists of 3–4 eggs. Arndt's second caution is to disbelieve texts that say that this species will colony breed. He is emphatically against this practice because bickering between pairs cannot be avoided.

Kremer found that parents have raised clutches in nestboxes ranging in size from 23cm square x 25cm high, to boxes measuring 25cm square x 50cm high, all with a 6cm diameter entrance hole.

Since the species are of similar size, Robben houses her Golden-crowned Conures and Painted Conures P. *p. picta* in the same sized cages and provides the same sized nestboxes. The cages measuring 122cm long x 61cm wide x 76cm high are double stacked. The nestbox can either be a cockatiel style box measuring 23cm square x 30cm high, or a boot-shaped box measuring 20cm square x 56cm high. Robben offers the pairs a choice of nestbox. The boxes are attached to the upper section of the outside of the cage.

Robben's pairs usually lay 3–4 eggs. She observes that 'the hen does all the sitting but the cock joins her at night.' Robben continues, 'When breeding, they don't seem as aggressive as the *Pyrrhuras*, and will tolerate quick nestbox checks, provided the birds are then left alone.' Incubation lasts approximately 25 days and young fledge between 7–8 weeks of age. Newly hatched have white down.

JANDAY CONURE
*Aratinga jandaya*

P ODEKERKEN

# JANDAY CONURE
## *Aratinga jandaya*

### Terminology

The Janday Conure *A. jandaya*, is also known as the Jendaya or Jandaya Conure and the Yellow-headed Conure. Some taxonomists believe the Janday Conure to be a separate species *A. jandaya*. Others list it as *A. auricapilla jandaya*, a subspecies of the Golden-capped (or Golden-headed) Conure. Low describes two colour variations. According to Kremer, *Jandaya* is taken from the South American Indian name for this bird but he offers no translation.

### Introduction and Pet Quality

The Janday Conure is one of the most colourful and affectionate of all the *Aratingas*. Unfortunately, these attributes are tempered by its loud, harsh voice. Do not make the mistake of judging its vocal abilities by its small stature, or by comparing it to the other *Aratinga* members of similar size. The intensity of the call may not, however, be as troublesome when the conures are housed in an outdoor aviary. If you are considering housing your birds outdoors, consult your neighbours first or be prepared for complaints.

Although this species has a reputation for being a destructive gnawer by nature, Kremer believes that this urge varies with the individual. In any event, it is wise to take steps to protect your prized possessions and valued furnishings, and whatever else is within your conure's reach. To keep these birds content, stockpile chewing branches and lots of toys.

Brenna Polk, Kam Pelham-Polk's daughter, prefers the Janday Conure over the Sun Conure *A. solstitialis*. She believes that they are calmer, not as highly strung, and extremely affectionate.

*Janday and Sun Conure chicks. This photograph shows the difference between the Sun and the Janday Conure. Unlike the Janday that has green wings, the adult Sun Conure's wing is yellow on the upper portion. The Sun Conure chick, on the right, shows the yellowing of the wing.*

Pelham-Polk is equally enamoured with them. 'They absolutely love to cuddle while maintaining an independent attitude. They are extremely intelligent and love to discover any and all new things.'

Pelham-Polk recommends housing Janday Conures in as large a cage as you can afford, one with 2cm x 2.5cm bar spacing. 'A large cage allows space for all of the toys and items needed to keep these little guys stimulated.'

June DiCiocco concurs that the Janday Conure is prized for its affection, especially the cock. This conure often favours the company of its human owner over that of its own kind – the ideal companion bird.

However, before throwing caution to the wind, DiCiocco warns that there are some hidden costs for having all this conure affection. A human-bonded Janday Conure can be overwhelming to some owners. Such a conure would love to be with you: that means they *love* to be *with you*, so you can expect to be summoned whenever your bird feels ignored. Those soliciting calls can become an irritant to someone without the time to dote on their bird.

Then there are those feelings of guilt you will go through when you have to leave your companion conure on its own from time to time. This need not be a huge concern. Your Janday Conure can easily amuse itself with its toys during your absence.

DiCiocco says that if you can manage a Janday Conure she can think of no good reason to discourage you from owning one.

## Description

Low describes the striking Janday Conure thus: 'It has the whole of the head, neck and part of the upper breast rich, bright yellow, merging into the rich red of the underparts. The thighs are olive-green sometimes marked with a few red feathers. The upperparts are green except for the lower back which is orange-red. The flight feathers and the tip of the tail are bright blue, the rest of the tail being bronze-green and the underside blackish. The bill is black and the iris is greyish brown.' The length is 30cm and the weight is approximately 110–125 grams.

The Janday Conure comes with either a white or a dark eye ring. Low states that the form with the paler eye ring also comes with 'more yellow than orange on the underparts.' Kremer has found that this is not always so. Arndt questions whether the slight colour variations point to their being a subspecies. It is unfortunate that so little is known about them in the wild.

At first glance, it is easy to confuse the Janday Conure with the Sun Conure *A. solstitialis*. However, on closer observation, it is impossible to confuse them. The upper back and wings of the Janday Conure are mostly green. (The back and wings of the Sun Conure are primarily yellow with dark blue in the large primary flight feathers and only hints of green on the secondaries.) The Janday Conure has a richer orange colouring. Consider too that the Janday Conure tends to have a smoother appearance than the scruffier looking Sun Conure due to the variations of colour all over this species especially prior to adulthood.

## In the Wild

Like the Queen of Bavaria's Conure *G. guarouba*, the Janday Conure inhabits north-eastern Brazil in South America. Their range includes the Brazilian mountains and regions of bush and low trees. Herman Kremer notes that in all areas, the climate is hot and wet with short dry periods and temperatures can be as high as 40°C and as low as 10°C in any one day.

Unlike the Queen of Bavaria's Conure that is very rarely viewed in the wild, the Janday Conure is quite commonly sighted.

Consequently, they are not believed to be in immediate danger of extinction. Apparently, the Janday Conure adapts to human encroachment on its range.

This species tends to flock in groups of up to 20 birds with coconut trees their regular haunt. They feast on seeds, berries and other fruits and a reasonable amount of greenery (to gnaw on).

Surprisingly, little is known about their nesting sites or their mating behaviour. As Kremer points out, this may be because breeding pairs withdraw from the flock and 'isolate themselves.'

## Breeding

The Janday Conure becomes sexually mature usually by the end of its second year. Nestboxes regularly used measure 30cm square x 55cm high with an 8cm diameter entrance hole, although Kremer has had success using a smaller box measuring 24cm long x 27cm wide x 53cm high with an entrance hole closer to 7cm in diameter. Kremer suggests housing pairs separately rather than maintaining a breeding colony as doing so imitates their wild behaviour.

DiCiocco's experience is to expect two clutches per year, 3–4 eggs per clutch, with a 100% hatchout as the rule. Her breeder pairs are 'excellent parents,' removing that particular worry from breeding this species. She pulls her chicks between 2–3 weeks of age for handfeeding.

To bring her birds into breeding mode, DiCiocco's prescription is to spike their diet with a protein boost by adding protein rich breeder pellets and scrambled eggs to their daily diet. (Remember to wean the adult birds off the protein boost after the breeding season, when the chicks have been removed.)

PELHAM-POLK

*Janday Conure chick at five weeks of age.*

DiCiocco also ensures that a water bath is always on hand.

Kam Pelham-Polk does not find it necessary to offer a breeding diet boost to her breeding pairs at the onset of the mating season. Obviously, her birds manage quite well on their own without it. Each year her breeders lay two to three clutches of between 3–5 eggs (three being common). However, before counting on a 100% survival rate of all the chicks that hatch, note that Pelham-Polk has found that Janday Conures will usually only take care of three or four babies. Any more than that and you should be prepared for handfeeding from day one. The adults tend to raise only the older chicks. She generally pulls the parent raised babies at 2–2 1/2 weeks of age for handfeeding.

As you may have surmised, Pelham-Polk does not recommend this species for the novice breeder. She has found them to be skittish during the breeding season. 'If disturbed too much, they can leave the nest, leaving the eggs to die.' To avoid potential egg abandonment, Pelham-Polk suggests giving each breeding pair plenty of privacy, out of sight but within hearing of other members of this group. Pelham-Polk's main concern is that the novice breeder will become discouraged by the challenges of Janday

Conure breeding, and thus may 'dump them for something a bit easier.'

To breed this conure Pelham-Polk recommends a cage measuring at least 61cm square x 91.5cm long with a nestbox 25.5cm square x 40.5cm high. (When one pair broke their eggs while moving around in this average sized nestbox, Pelham-Polk substituted a smaller, boot-shaped box and the next clutch of eggs was not damaged.) Pelham-Polk offers these tips regarding the nestbox: 'They toss every single bit of material out of the box and lay their eggs on the bare floor of the box. Once the first egg is laid, more bedding should be placed under the eggs to help prevent damage. Once the first chick is hatched, add more bedding to ensure their safety. The hen incubates the eggs with the cock guarding the nesting area. They sleep in their box all year round.'

DiCioccio has success with a small ABS hard plastic nestbox measuring 23cm wide x 20.5cm deep x 56cm high in the shape of a grandfather clock. 'With ABS plastic boxes, they don't toss out their aspen nesting/bedding material.' Her birds roost in their nestbox all year round.

Incubation is approximately 23 days with fledging between 7–8 weeks of age. Although some breeders such as Robben say their chicks hatch with white down, DiCiocco insists her chicks hatch with pale yellow down.

PELHAM-POLK

*Janday Conure chick at six weeks of age.*

**SUN CONURE**
*Aratinga solstitialis*

P ODEKERKEN

# SUN CONURE
## *Aratinga solstitialis*

### Terminology

Low and Arndt refer to the Sun Conure, also commonly known as the Yellow Conure, as *A. auricapilla solstitialis*, a subspecies of the Golden-capped Conure *Aratinga auricapilla auricapilla*, along with the Janday Conure *A. auricapilla jandaya*. One cannot help but notice the similarities between the Sun Conure and the Janday Conure.

Kremer, on the other hand, follows Joseph Forshaw's classification namely that the Sun Conure *A. solstitialis* is a separate species (as is the Janday Conure *A. jandaya*). Interestingly, the natural habitats of the Sun Conure *A. solstitialis* and the Janday Conure *A. jandaya* are separated by a large stretch of land ie, their territory does not overlap. (The Janday Conure *A. jandaya* habitat is, however, relatively close to that of the Golden-capped Conure *A. a. auricapilla*, but their habitats still do not overlap.) *Solstitialis* means 'pertaining to the solstice'. (*Sol* means 'sun'.)

### Introduction and Pet Quality

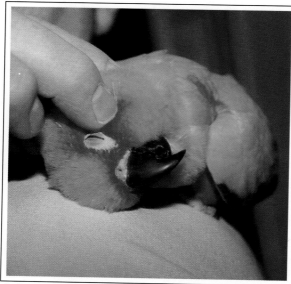

*A Sun Conure enjoying a head scratch.*

The Sun Conure personifies both the positive and negative extremes of conure keeping. Arguably, these conures are the most appealing to the eye and have one of the most charming personalities and yet, they can be the most unpleasant to the ear of all the conures of the genus *Aratinga*. However, do not despair or cross them off your want list just yet. Arndt observed that the tamer the Sun Conure is, the quieter it is, vocalising only when disturbed, and at dawn and dusk.

Bob and Wendy Wilson of Saxe Point Aviary are enthusiastic breeders of Sun Conures. They rave about their 'amazing colours,' their intelligence which they feel is comparable to that of the larger parrots, and their captivating personality. The Wilsons believe that Sun Conures can be trained to be no louder than any of the larger parrots. However, they do caution that the keeping of this species is more of a challenge than the keeping of the Maroon-bellied Conure *Pyrrhura frontalis*, also in their collection. They state that Sun Conures are larger, more demanding and louder. Their cage must be of strong construction. They also enjoy rope toys and large copper bells, and need to have a variety of dog bone or rope toys to destroy!

It is beginning to become clear why Sun Conures are so addictive to own despite their potential for noise. It is their personality: their charm; their gentle and friendly disposition; and their *joie de vivre*, whether at play alone, together with their own kind, or with their keepers. The Wilsons, whose collection also includes Nanday Conures

*Nandayas nenday*, say that all their conures seem to be birds that enjoy being held and snuggled, and that this is particularly true of Sun Conures. 'All of our conures are very amusing to watch at play. They are very good at amusing themselves. However, a handfed chick, if it is to be kept content and less vocal, must have a regular playtime with its keeper.'

*Sun Conure adult with James Taylor. (Please note that the authors discourage allowing a parrot on the shoulder.)*

To view this splendid species to advantage, Arndt suggests housing them in an outdoor aviary. (The Wilsons urge giving conures ample flying room in the aviary, with a flight cage measuring 1.2 metres long x 1.2 metres wide x 1.8 metres high as a bare minimum.) Once acclimatised to the outdoors, these birds are quite hardy provided that they have access to a frost-free area in winter.

## Description

Low, who claims that the Sun Conure is 'a bird of quite exceptional beauty,' describes it thus: 'The plumage is variable, it is mainly yellow and orange or a fiery shade of orange-red, with most of the yellow areas tinged with

*Above: A Sun Conure at six months of age.*
*Right: A Sun Conure at nine months of age.*

orange. The head and underparts are fiery orange and the wings are yellow with the secondaries partly green. The primaries are dark blue and the tail is olive-green, sometimes blue on the outer webs of the feathers. The undertail coverts are green tinged with yellow and the underside of the tail is dusky olive. The bill is black and the periorbital skin is whitish.' The length is 30cm and the weight is approximately 100–120 grams.

## In the Wild

Sun Conures flock in small and large groups in areas north of the Amazon River in north-eastern South America. Their habitat is the warm damp climate of the tropical and subtropical grasslands containing scattered trees or savannahs, woods of palm trees and the open woods to an altitude of 1200 metres. They nest in holes in palm and other trees. Although little is known of their habits in the wild, Kremer surmises that, like other *Aratinga* members, they feed on fruits, nuts, seeds, insects and insect larvae. Forshaw quotes sightings of this species feeding on fruits and seeds.

A wild flock of brilliantly coloured, screaming Sun Conures alighting in a fruit plantation, although it might be a parrot watcher's dream, is undoubtedly many a farmer's nightmare.

## Breeding

Arndt believes the Sun Conure to be one of the easiest of the *Aratinga* genus to breed.

For the breeder without concern about sound levels, the Sun Conure is a delightful bird not only for its striking colour but also for its enjoyment of the aviary environment, say the Wilsons. 'We would not advise colony breeding Sun Conures, however, as they are very territorial.' As with all their conures, a nestbox is provided for roosting year round. Additionally, as with their house pet conures, those housed in the aviary are also provided with toys to keep them amused.

Kremer finds that the Sun Conure attains adult plumage by approximately 18 months of age and are sexually mature at approximately two years. With the approach of the breeding season, the pair mate regularly and the hen becomes more and more recluse in the nestbox. The reclusive behaviour of the hen with the company of the cock is a better indication of breeding because mating – serving mainly to strengthen the

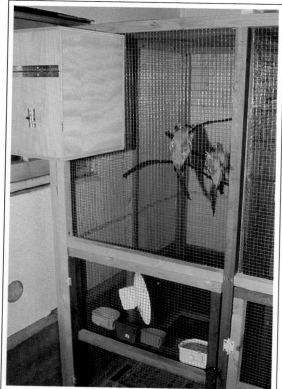

*Sun Conure breeding flight at Saxe Point Aviary.*

pair bond – can occur without eggs being produced. The eggs are laid on a nest of splintered wood chewed by the adults during seclusion in the nestbox.

Kremer suggests removing weaned chicks from their parents' flight because the chicks will roost with their parents in the nestbox at night and thus risk damaging the second clutch of eggs if laid.

A variety of nestbox sizes have been used successfully. These include dimensions of 30cm square x 45cm high, 45cm square x 120cm high, 25cm square x 40cm high with an 8cm diameter entrance hole and 18cm square x 46cm high with a 7cm diameter entrance hole.

Robben's hens lay an average of four eggs (as many as six eggs have been reported by other breeders), and says that the hens could lay as many clutches as allowed. She, however, only allows her hens to clutch three times a year. The Wilsons, Taylor, DiCiocco and Robben all agree that egg fertility rate is very good, that incubation for this species is approximately 23–25 days, and that chicks fledge at 7–8 weeks of age. Most

P ODEKERKEN

*Sun Conure nestling.*

breeders expect yellow down at hatching. However Robben states, 'When the chicks first hatch the initial down is white, then they fill in with a yellowish-coloured down'.

ABK

*Pair of Sun Conures.*

**DUSKY-HEADED CONURE**
*Aratinga weddellii*

P ODEKERKEN

# DUSKY-HEADED CONURE
*Aratinga weddellii*

## Terminology

The Dusky-headed Conure *A. weddellii* is also commonly called the Dusky Conure. It is also known as the Weddell's Conure honouring Dr. Hugh Algernon Weddell, a naturalist who led a French expedition to South America in the mid-nineteenth century.

## Introduction and Pet Quality

The Dusky-headed Conure is the favourite species at the Casagrande's Rain Coast Aviary where they specialise in the breeding of numerous species of conures, many of which have qualified for First Breeder certificates (Canada). This species is, for them, the most undervalued of the conures. The reason for this is undoubtedly their lack of brilliant plumage colouration. The Casagrandes, however, say that you just have to get to know one to fall in love with them. They are very charming and relatively quiet too – for a conure, that is.

Their quietness must account for why they are not considered to be great talkers. 'Some of our birds say a few words. They make up for any lack of speaking ability with their sweetness of nature', explains Janet Casagrande.

Like Casagrande, June DiCiocco highly recommends the Dusky-headed Conure as a pet, and not merely because of its restrained utterances. 'The Dusky Conure is a pint-sized bundle of sweetness and will easily win you over.' DiCiocco describes her own birds: 'Their favourite behaviour is to hang upside down in the cage in the bat position. They will also lie in the palm of your hand on their backs while you scratch their bellies.'

DiCiocco reminds us that as with *Aratingas* in general, they do have the urge to chew and must be provided an ample supply of branches and chewable toys.

Kremer agrees that Dusky-headed Conures are not very noisy, and points out that they only use their full voices when disturbed or when they call for a short time in the morning and evening. Arndt concurs, saying that they are unique as *Aratingas* in

*Dusky-headed Conure chick.*

that they hardly ever use their piercing voices except under extreme excitement. Like the Casagrandes, Arndt believes that their quiet, timid nature explains their reluctance to talk.

Arndt concludes that their quiet nature makes them especially suitable for an outdoor aviary particularly since they will survive some frost. Kremer agrees that this species is cold hardy.

## Description

Low describes the Dusky-headed Conure as being 'recognised by the pale grey iris and the greyish blue appearance of the head. There is a broad area of white skin surrounding the eye. The plumage is mainly green, more yellowish on the abdomen. The tail is tipped with blue and the outer webs of the primaries and secondaries are blue. The bill is black.' The length is 28cm and the weight approximately 115 grams.

This conure does not have bright colouration but what it lacks in appearance is more than made up for in its personality.

*Dusky-headed Conure chick at ten weeks of age.*

## In the Wild

The Dusky-headed Conure ranges over the huge area of the western Amazon River basin, from as far north as Colombia, through eastern Peru, Bolivia and western Brazil in South America. It is common in the stands of trees along the river, within open savannahs and along mountain sides. According to Kremer, this species is a lowland bird living in flocks of up to approximately 20 individuals.

For an apparently common bird with a stable population, surprisingly little is known about it in the wild.

## Breeding

DiCiocco finds that handraised Dusky-headed Conures are sexually mature between two and three years of age. DiCiocco warns that they do get flighty in an aviary and can be nervous breeders although they are good parents and tend to double clutch in nestboxes measuring 20cm square x 56cm high.

Kremer gives a variety of nestbox sizes that have been used successfully: 15cm square x 47cm high, 30cm square x 50cm high, 40cm square x 60cm high, 24cm square x 30cm high, 25cm square x 75cm high and 28cm square x 45cm high with an entrance hole of 7cm diameter. Kremer also mentions a British breeder whose pairs preferred their nestbox complete with a 15cm long entrance tunnel, hung crookedly.

Here is another Kremer tip for breeding. To stimulate the start of breeding, place pieces of half rotten wood in the box for the hen to chew prior to laying her eggs. Two to four eggs are the norm. DiCiocco reports an incubation period of approximately 23 days. Chicks hatch with whitish down and a black-tipped beak. DiCiocco also says that chicks fledge between 7–8 weeks of age whether parent raised or handfed. Kremer agrees.

*Dusky-headed Conure on cage door.*

**PATAGONIAN CONURE**
*Cyanoliseus patagonus*

P ODEKERKEN

# PATAGONIAN CONURE
## *Cyanoliseus patagonus*

### Terminology

*C. patagonus* known simply as the Patagonian Conure or Burrowing Parrot, is the only member of the *Cyanoliseus* genus. No doubt the name 'Patagonian' is taken from the southern regions of Argentina known as Patagonia, where this conure is found.

### Introduction and Pet Quality

Sandi Brennan, of Fine Feathered Flock Aviary loves Patagonian Conures. *Mystic* is the first Patagonian Conure to endear himself to her by faking a 'sneeze' to get her attention. An avian veterinarian diagnosed *Mystic's* 'sneeze' as solicitation behaviour. The mischievous conure's name was then changed to *Diablo* ('devil' in Spanish). His antics certainly amuse Brennan: 'That nutty bird hangs from his cage by his beak with his legs pointing down and his wings fluttering. He dances and struts and stomps in a manner unlike any other conure I've seen. He lets me pet him anywhere and will let me hold him, on his back, in the palm of my hand. He usually will allow anyone to pet him or hold him.'

Moodiness, however, eventually caused *Diablo* to become a problem pet. Brennan chose to place him in a breeding program. *Diablo*, by the way, did not pair with the first hen presented. In fact, he waited for the third hen. (His chosen hen is as moody as he is.)

'I think my problem with *Diablo* was as much conure adolescence as lack of attention. As I look back, I was accumulating too many pets but did not have enough time during that period. I have since learned that adolescence can be managed with time, love and patience', explains Brennan.

The International Conure Association's newsletter quoted that handraised Patagonian Conure chicks make delightful pets. Brennan agrees, saying that properly trained these birds are hard to beat as a pet. 'They will talk quite well, love to cuddle and will entertain themselves with toys when you are busy. Another interesting thing about these conures is that they love to get on the floor and follow you.'

PELHAM-POLK

*Brenna Polk with a four month old Patagonian Conure.*

Low also regards the Patagonian Conure favourably. 'Its pleasing colouration and proportions make it, in my view, one of the most desirable of the parrakeets from South America.'

Nine of Brennan's pairs are wild however, and shy away from view during the day. Interestingly, they make their presence known on moon filled nights. 'Our aviary has very large skylights, one of which is directly above the colony cage. On nights when the moon is nearly full they are very active and fairly noisy.' With their breeding aviary dimly lit, they 'can be heard feeding their babies far into the night.'

## Description

This species cannot be confused with any other conure. The Patagonian Conure, says Low, 'is a large and beautiful conure of elegant proportions' and can be distinguished from most other conures by its feathered cere.

Low continues her description: 'The head, neck and back are dark olive-brown tinged with green; the throat and breast are

PELHAM-POLK

*Patagonian Conure.*

greyish brown, with some white on the upper breast. There is an area of bright red and yellow on the abdomen: the centre and the thighs are orange-red, the rest of the abdomen, also the rump and uppertail coverts being yellow. The wings are olive-green with the primaries and primary coverts blue. The upper surface of the tail is olive-green, the central feathers having a bluish tinge along the middle; the under surface is brown and the undertail coverts are olive-yellow. The beak is black and the iris is white. An area of bare white skin surrounds the eye.' The length is 45cm and the weight is approximately 280 grams.

## In the Wild

Patagonian Conures are found primarily in Argentina, South America. Forshaw notes that these conures were once widespread in central Chile but due to their being shot as pests and the chicks being regarded as a delicacy, their numbers have declined drastically. The bird is now legally protected in Chile. In Argentina these birds appear to be more common although, here too, their numbers have been reduced by human activity.

According to Forshaw, this species inhabits open country especially along streams and rivers. Seasonal migration does occur: the availability of food seems to be the motivating factor for this movement. Most of their daily activity comprises foraging for seeds and fruits. To roost, the birds gather from all directions into a grove of trees or flock to burrows that they have dug in sandstone cliff faces. They settle down long after dark and have been known to fly at night and before dusk.

Their habit of burrowing into sandstone cliffs distinguishes the Patagonian from other conures. The nest chambers may be at the end of a very long tunnel (of up to 3 metres). They nest in colonies with their tunnels often zigzagging across each other to form a communal network of caves. It is no wonder, therefore, that this conure is nicknamed the 'Burrowing Parrot,' and the 'Cliff-dwelling Parrot.'

Amazingly, birds enter these tunnels at full flight, closing their wings just before the cliff face and whooshing into the entrance for a landing on the run.

## Breeding

Three or four eggs per clutch, with one or two clutches per year, is Brennan's current breeding experience. In October 1992, Brennan chose to experiment with colony breeding these conures at her breeding complex. Since she knew they would breed communally in the wild, she thought it worth trying because the traditional stacked breeding-cage method was proving unsatisfactory.

For a fresh start, the birds were individually sexed and marked (on their feathers) for identification. All the birds were assembled together and allowed to select their own mate, to form natural pairs. Ironically, it was only after moulting (thus having discarded Brennan's identification markings) that they formed into seven breeding pairs.

The communal flight was assembled on the inside of Brennan's breeding facility. The flight consisted of two free-standing 1.2 metre square x 2.4 metre long flights attached together along one side. Holes through the adjoining wall allowed the birds full access to both flights. Ten nestboxes were hung along the top, on the outside of this colony enclosure, away from the food serving area. Each nestbox entrance hole was at the same height. 'The boxes are horizontal measuring 30cm square x 61cm long. I put in coarse pine shavings which they chewed to powder prior to nesting. My wild-caught Patagonian Conures generally live in their nestbox or at the very least dive in when we are in the building.'

Three of the seven pairs nested just four months later, in February 1993. This,

*Patagonian Conure in breeding aviary.*

surprisingly, was outside of the birds' normal nesting season of late spring and early summer. One pair, however, 'remembered to wait until spring.'

Not wanting to tempt fate, all the eggs were pulled for artificial incubation a week before their estimated hatch date. Those chicks were handreared. 'Exhaustion made me leave the second clutches. All the eggs hatched and were fed by the parents without incident.'

Personal circumstances have since ended that experiment. As for what conclusions were drawn, Brennan says, 'I will never know if colony breeding is viable over time. My personal belief is that it is.' Incidentally, two of those pairs produced clutches after being relocated from the breeding colony and housed as individual pairs in traditional stacked breeding cages.

Brennan has found that wild, shy birds retreat into the corner of their nestbox during inspections whereas handraised birds attack nestbox intruders. 'They will back up to the far end of their box and charge. Last year, this resulted in broken eggs.' Caution is therefore advisable.

Brennan says to expect Patagonian Conure chicks to be noisy during handrearing. They make a 'beeping' sound when only two-thirds empty and stomp their feet when wanting to be fed. Even after feeding, they take some time before settling down to sleep (often sleeping on their back!). And if you value your birds' feather appearance, Brennan recommends housing the chicks individually. 'They enjoy rough and tumble play so much that it is hard to separate them, but if you want them to have neat tails and smooth feathers you should. I also suggest teaching the 'step up' command at a young age or they will act like a mule when presented with a hand later.'

Incubation lasts for a period of approximately 24–25 days. Young fledge at approximately eight weeks of age.

QUEEN OF BAVARIA'S
CONURE
*Guaruba guarouba*

P ODEKERKEN

# QUEEN OF BAVARIA'S CONURE
## *Guaruba guarouba*

## Terminology

The Queen of Bavaria's Conure *G. guarouba* is also commonly known as the Golden Conure, or simply as the Queen Conure. To further confuse things, it is listed in the USA's Endangered Species Act as the Golden Parrakeet.

We have been unable to determine the reason for the common name Queen of Bavaria's Conure. On the other hand, from Kremer we learned that the term *guarouba* comes from the South American Indian word meaning 'yellow bird', which is very appropriate! Since the word 'golden' is used in the common name of a number of conures, it is a pity that this conure could not have been named simply the Guarouba Conure!

Until very recently, the Queen of Bavaria's Conure *G. guarouba* was classified as *Aratinga guarouba* (and still is by some taxonomists).

## Introduction and Pet Quality

Without a doubt the Queen of Bavaria's Conure is a highly desirable bird. It is stunningly beautiful with, as Low describes it, 'abundant intelligence and playfulness.' Kremer notes that these conures can be very tame and affectionate, unlike many of the *Aratinga* members, amongst which it was classified until recently. Arndt also admires their lovable character, delights in their curiosity and playfulness, and refers to his own bird singing 'aria-like in charming tones.' However, all three authors caution about this conure's three drawbacks without which it would make an ideal companion bird.

First, there is the matter of voice. Some of the words used to describe it are: loud, powerful, earsplitting, shrill, metallic, nerve splitting – you get the idea.

The second drawback is this species' tendency to feather pluck. Again, all three authors mention this unfortunate behaviour. Although it is not known why these conures do this, their feather plucking behaviour appears to be linked to their need, as highly intelligent and curious creatures, for stimuli and distraction. Low feels that 'they require more attention than the average person can provide.' DiCiocco has found that 'if fed properly and kept in humid conditions [thus imitating their natural environment of the rainforest], a pair can remain in good feather in the aviary. In my opinion, the hen will pick her tail feathers out to make it easier for the cock to copulate with her.'

The third problem is their rarity both in captivity and in the wild where their habitat has been decimated, and therefore this species is expensive. Consequently the Queen of Bavaria's Conure is often bought solely as a status symbol. Arndt believes that because these conures are so endangered, they should only be in the hands of breeders dedicated to increasing stocks for other breeders. DiCiocco agrees, saying that 'they were noted as becoming increasingly rare as far back as 1946. Therefore, although the bird is playful and would make a good pet, it should remain in the hands of the experienced aviculturist.'

Even though these conures are not recommended as pet birds, they can be thoroughly enjoyed as aviary specimens. Low claims that viewing a pair at play in an aviary 'is one of the most pleasing sights imaginable.'

## Description

Low describes this species thus: 'The Queen of Bavaria's Conure is rich golden yellow throughout, except for the green primaries and secondary flight feathers. The massive beak (light horn-coloured) and short, tapered tail, contribute to the top-heavy

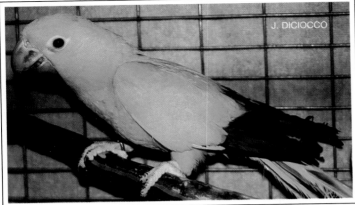

appearance.' The length is 36cm and weight approximately 230 grams.

Arndt notes that hens are often as large as cocks and sometimes larger.

*Juvenile Queen of Bavaria's Conure. Until recently it was classified as Aratinga guarouba.*

## In the Wild

The Queen of Bavaria's Conure is native to the jungles of northern Brazil that run parallel to the southern shores of the Amazon River in South America. Their habitat is equatorial tropical rainforest.

They gather in flocks of 6–30 birds. As would be expected, flock numbers rise and fall during and after the breeding season which, according to Arndt, appears to be in autumn. Individual pairs go off to nest in private. When they return, their offspring join the flock.

This species forages in the rainforest canopy on fruits, berries, seeds and nuts. Arndt notes that pairs nest in tree cavities approximately 10 metres above ground. Two or three eggs are normally laid and the hen takes incubation seriously. The cock only incubates when the hen is off the nest, which is for short periods of time. Chick feeding, however, is a mutual affair with both parents sharing the duty. When the chicks fledge the family then joins the main flock.

When feeling threatened, the adult expresses itself visually through postures or dances using, as Kremer describes them, 'a wide range of expressive movements: bill-tapping, beating of the wings, spreading the tail, swaying the head from side to side, putting the head under the wing, walking back and forth along a branch, etc.'

Very little is known about their habits in the wild because there have been no field studies until recently. Fortunately, the World Parrot Trust has established a fund and launched a field study of the Queen of Bavaria's Conure. At the time of printing this book the results of that study were not available.

Sadly, these fascinating creatures are rarely seen in the wild. This is due to habitat destruction by humans and the bird's inability to adapt to change.

## Breeding

With such a rare bird, it is foolish to take risks regarding their housing and breeding. This species has been found to be cold hardy and capable of adapting to colder climates.

(Kremer claims that they can tolerate low temperatures as long as they have a nestbox to roost in overnight.) However, risk of injury from frost is too high not to provide them with a heated shelter if they are housed in an outdoor aviary in colder climates. Although they get along amicably in the company of other birds outside the breeding season, once breeding commences they can be ruthless aggressors regardless of the size of the birds being attacked. Therefore, pairs should be housed separately. (Arndt suggests that colony breeding will be unsuccessful because the playfulness of these birds distracts them from the serious pursuit of breeding.) Little precaution is necessary for the aviary as this species is not as destructive to a timber structure as the *Aratinga* species might be, however provision should be made to ensure that the ambient humidity never drops too low. It must be remembered that these birds originate from the thick of the tropical rainforest.

To prepare the Queen of Bavaria's Conure for breeding, the dimensions of their flight should ideally measure 2 metres square x 4 metres long. Some breeders have been successful with a nestbox measuring 23cm square x 60cm high. Arndt notes that they should readily accept a hollow tree trunk or other nestbox size provided that these are at least 35cm in diameter.

DiCiocco houses her breeding pairs in cages measuring 1.2 metres square x 2.4 metres long, furnished with hardwood perches. 'This is a minimum size for a pair of these larger conures. I use a nestbox measuring 30cm square x 71cm deep, which is grandfather clock shaped. In the winter they can withstand cold climates if they use the nestbox to roost in at night.'

Mating takes place in what Kremer astutely labels as 'typical South American fashion.' The cock clings to the hen's back with one foot, while the other foot remains on the perch to balance him. (We have observed our South American Maximilian's Pionus Parrots *Pionus maximiliani maximiliani* mating this way.)

When you see mating behaviour, it is time to check stock for handfeeding formula and leg bands, and collect your armour, or at least be vigilant for aggressive behaviour. Kremer says that even the keeper is at risk of being attacked at this time. Therefore, do not take it personally if you receive a bite or you are rejected during the mating season. The individual birds will return to normal when the chicks have been pulled for handfeeding. If chicks are left to be raised by their parents, usually they are ready to leave the nestbox after ten weeks. Arndt cautions that this species is very sensitive to nest inspection. 'Many a clutch was abandoned because of the owner's excessive curiosity, or the young were no longer fed.'

J. DICIOCCO

Based on her experience, DiCiocco confirms that in captivity you can expect the average clutch to be 4–6 eggs and that the eggs are incubated between 26–28 days. The chicks hatch with white fluff which they lose. Fledging occurs at approximately 9–10 weeks of age.

Kremer notes an added bonus to breeding the Queen of Bavaria's Conure is that the chicks can be left with their parents for up to three years. Imagine all those generations in a flight. Think of the unusual opportunity to watch and to study their flock dynamics.

*Young Queen of Bavaria's Conures in their cage.*

**NANDAY CONURE**
*Nandayus nenday*

P ODEKERKEN

# NANDAY CONURE
## *Nandayus nenday*

### Terminology

The Nanday Conure *N. nenday* is also commonly called the Black-headed Conure and the Black-masked Conure.

Like the Patagonian Conure *C. patagonus* and the Queen of Bavaria's Conure *G. guarouba*, the Nanday Conure is classified in a genus of its own. Many aviculturists, such as the Wilsons, find the Nanday Conure so similar to the Sun Conure *A. solstitialis* that they believe both conures should be in the same genus classification of *Aratinga*. Even Low feels that the Nanday Conure should be included with the genus *Aratinga*, because of its similarity to *Aratinga* behaviour and need for care. 'It is difficult to see how minor anatomical differences can justify placing it in a separate genus,' she comments.

### Introduction and Pet Quality

Do you enjoy a challenge? Would you love to own a conure but you are on a tight budget? Can you tolerate some high-spirited loudness in your life? Do you have free access to a constant supply of twigs for your bird's cage or flight? Are you handy at replacing and repairing wooden nestboxes and the exposed wooden areas of your aviary? If the answer to all these questions is yes, then perhaps the Nanday Conure is for you.

Anyone seeking more of a conure keeping challenge than, say, owning an undemanding Maroon-bellied Conure *P. frontalis*, should consider this species, advise Bob and Wendy Wilson of Saxe Point Aviary. According to the Wilsons, the Nanday Conure's strong beak and avid need to gnaw is the challenge to keeping this conure, not its reputation for being loud. To prevent them from chewing the aviary and nestbox into a pile of wood chips is a real challenge. 'They appear to be more destructive than Sun Conures [*Aratinga solstitialis*] and will chew just for fun, not simply in preparation for breeding,' explains the Wilsons.

Additionally, if this species is to be housed in a cage, the Wilsons urge choosing a cage sturdy enough to resist the strong beak of a much larger parrot. They warn to expect toys to be chewed to pieces within a very short time.

So what of this bird's reputation for loudness? Arndt, in fact, insinuates that they are amongst the loudest of all the South American conures. 'No problem!' says Wendy Wilson who has solved the problem by training her Nanday Conures to whisper instead of shout. Now, what would have been a raucous cheer as they greet the day and settle in for the night, is but a whispered chorus. Even their alarm calls

*Nanday Conure.*

are restrained. It can be done!

Although the Nanday Conure has a loud sound and piercing voice, one cannot overlook the visual appeal and fascinating personality of these fine feathered creatures. 'Their appearance contains a contradiction,' says Wendy Wilson, 'they are plain green with a twist.' She feels that their black bandit face mask is in contrast to its casual red socks. The Wilsons also find that their Nanday Conures have as much personality and charm as their Sun Conures. They say the trick to keeping chicks content and less vocal is to allow them a regular playtime.

## Description

Its black cap and face mask along with its red thighs make the Nanday Conure stand out in the crowd. Low describes it thus: 'The throat and upper breast are washed with blue. The upper surface of the tail is green edged with blue, the underside being blackish. The outer webs of the flight feathers are blue. The remainder of the plumage is green, more yellowish below, also on the lower back, rump and underwing coverts. The bill is black and the iris is dark brown. There is a narrow circle of whitish skin surrounding the eye.' It weighs approximately 140 grams. The length is 31cm, half of this being the tail measurement.

## In the Wild

The Nanday Conure is common, travelling in large flocks, and is found in open areas in its rather small 200km wide territory through south-eastern Bolivia, Brazil, Paraguay and northern Argentina in South America. This is another parrot species that seems to be benefiting from the encroachment of humans into their territory. It is, as Low and Forshaw point out, often found feeding on crops of maize and sunflower and nesting in fence posts.

## Breeding

The Wilsons find that their Nanday Conures enjoy an aviary atmosphere. However, contrary to Low's belief, the Wilsons do not advise colony breeding as this species is very territorial.

As with all their conures, the Wilsons provide a nestbox at all times, breeding season or not. (Their conures roost in their nestbox year round.) The cages they provide measure 1.25 metres wide x 1.25 metres long x 1.9 metres high. The more space the better, they say. Toys are provided for the amusement of their breeding birds as well as for their house pets.

The nestbox is constructed of 2cm pine boards and is replaced when damaged beyond repair or when soiled. The box is placed in an accessible but secluded high position in the aviary, away from the feeding area. The nestbox measures 31cm square x 47cm deep with a 5cm diameter entrance hole. For this size of conure, providing a slightly smaller entrance hole will stimulate the pair to breed, as they need to chew their way into the nestbox. (Note: for smaller and less avid chewing species of conures, an

entrance hole which is too small may hamper their entry into the box and encourage them to abandon their breeding.) Pine shavings are placed into the nestbox but this is quickly house-cleaned out of the box by the adult birds. Eggs are laid on the bare floor. The average clutch is 3–5 eggs. Robben concurs with the Wilsons regarding the incubation period being around 24 days and that the chicks fledge at approximately eight weeks of age. However, Robben says that her chicks hatch with white down whereas the Wilsons claim that their chicks hatch with grey-coloured down.

*Above:*
*Nanday Conures in flight at Saxe Point Aviary. The famous whispering Nandays.*

*Right:*
*Nanday Conure cock.*

P ODEKERKEN

**FIERY-SHOULDERED
CONURE**
*Pyrrhura egregia*

P ODEKERKEN

# FIERY-SHOULDERED CONURE
## *Pyrrhura egregia*

### Terminology
Also classified as *P. e. egregia* by some taxonomists, the Fiery-shouldered Conure is also commonly known as the Demerara Conure. The name *egregia* comes from the Latin word *egregius* meaning 'extraordinary'.

### Introduction and Pet Quality
'I think Fiery-shouldered Conures are very beautiful birds, in their looks as well as in their nature. At first I was interested in them only because of their rarity, and the fact that very few keepers in Canada and the USA kept them. Surprisingly, we have found them to be very free breeders. I think handraised young would make wonderful companion birds, but because their numbers are so low, I think we should concentrate on breeding for breeders,' explains Janet Casagrande.

The Casagrandes find Fiery-shouldered Conures relatively quiet and not at all destructive. However, they are not at all suitable for a communal aviary, as they are very aggressive towards other birds.

Don Harris agrees with the Casagrandes that this species is attractive, shows no signs of being destructive and are no more noisy than the average *Pyrrhura* member. He also adds that they are very intelligent birds and observes that the young birds are very shy.

### Description

P ODEKERKEN

Thomas Arndt's book *The Atlas of Conures* displays a spectacular illustration (by Arndt) of a Fiery-shouldered Conure in full display with wings outstretched and tail fanned. This conure has quite a theatrical appearance with its flaming underwing coverts and V-shaped dark-feathered fanned tail. The white eye ring is accentuated by its dark crown and forehead and reddish ear coverts. On closer observation the matching dark patch on its belly becomes apparent. Unusual for *Pyrrhura* members, it has a horn-coloured beak.

*The underwing of the Fiery-shouldered Conure.*

Low describes the Fiery-shouldered Conure thus: 'The most beautiful feature is the underwing coverts which are yellow and orange; the bend of the wing and the carpal edge are red. There is a narrow brown frontal band and the feathers of the top of the head are brown edged with green; the ear coverts are reddish brown. Feathers of the sides of the neck, throat and upper breast are green, narrowly edged with yellow or yellowish white. The centre of the abdomen is variably suffused with brownish red. The tail is dark maroon above, greyish below. The bill is horn-coloured (note this unusual feature) and the iris is brown.' The length is 25cm and weight is approximately 75 grams.

## In the Wild

The Fiery-shouldered Conure is a rare species. Little about its wild behaviour has been recorded, probably because of its rarity in nature. This spectacular parrot is believed to exist in the wild in a small area of South America, in the mountain regions bordering western Guyana and south-eastern Venezuela. Arndt says that they are only seen in single pairs, or in a small group, and usually high up in treetops. Arndt also reports that apparently this conure's way of life and behaviour is similar to that of the Painted Conure *P. p. picta*.

## Breeding

At Rain Coast Aviary, Janet and Brian Casagrande presented an opportunity to examine how this rare species is housed and bred in captivity. Their breeding pairs are housed separately. Each pair is housed in a spacious breeding cage measuring 61cm square x 91cm long which is constructed of heavy duty 25mm x 12.5mm aviary wire mesh. The breeding cages are suspended for ease of access and cleaning. They hang in two-tiered clusters on the inside walls of the facility. Pair privacy is ensured by blocking their view of each other, to avoid visual intimidation between pairs. 'This is a must,' says Brian Casagrande, 'especially with the Fiery-shouldered Conure.'

The aviary is equipped with full spectrum lighting for 'sunlight' and with night lights as a precaution against 'night fright' in the flock. In winter the aviary is heated to 15°C. Janet Casagrande questions the necessity for this by stating that the pairs roost in a sheltered nestbox. However, she dismisses her concern about heating costs by admitting that this may be the reason for their year round breeding success. The Casagrandes, by the way, have not heard of anyone housing these conures outdoors so they cannot vouch for their cold hardiness. In any case, note that this species' wild habitat is mountain regions located almost on the Equator, a very tropical climate.

The Casagrandes find their birds to be free breeders. Three clutches a year are normal with 3–6 chicks a possibility but with four chicks the average. Their pairs nest and roost in their nestbox. The nestbox measures 24cm square

*Four Fiery-shouldered Conures at five months of age at Rain Coast Aviary.*

x 35cm high with a 6cm diameter entrance hole. It is attached to the exterior end of the breeder cage away from food and water containers, so that the entrance hole is near the top of the cage. Pine wood chips are placed into the box for bedding or nest-making material. One of the Casagrande's breeding pairs clears the nestbox and the hen lays her eggs on the bare floor whereas the other pair welcome fresh nesting material. A word about the nestbox: Brian Casagrande warns against its removal after the breeding season (ie to dissuade the birds from breeding again) because the birds will experience stress at the loss of their year round roost.

The Casagrandes are in the midst of determining exactly what kind of parents these conures make. Four parent raised chicks are being allowed to remain with their parents beyond weaning. The chicks are now between 10–12 weeks of age. The parent birds, although under close supervision have proven to be excellent parents so far.

ABK

*Fiery-shouldered Conures on their nestbox.*

When the Casagrandes started out, all they could find out about the Fiery-shouldered Conure was that they do not get along with other birds. This proved to be true when two cock chicks were housed with two Dusky-headed Conures *A. weddellii* of approximately the same age. The Fiery- shouldered Conure chicks attacked the Dusky-headed Conure chicks 'like piranhas.' From that experience, Janet Casagrande is emphatic that Fiery-shouldered Conures can be vicious towards other birds. Happily, they are not aggressive toward their keepers.

Don Harris also houses his pairs separately in cages measuring 76cm wide x 61cm high x 91.5cm long. He provides them with a year-round nestbox measuring 20cm square x 61cm with a 6.5cm entrance hole. 'I supply pine shavings for nesting material. They chew this into fine bits. I clean out the nestbox and replenish as needed.' His pairs start to breed midwinter, laying 3–8 eggs with 100% fertility. On hatching, the chicks are a bright pink with thin, long grey down after 23–25 days incubation. They fledge at 6–7 weeks of age. Harris pulls his chicks for handrearing as early as 10 days of age only because of the rarity of this species in the USA.

A breeding tip from Harris: 'My Fiery-shouldered Conures seem to do better when within close sight and sound of other *Pyrrhura* species. But they require privacy from humans.' Although he has not closely observed the mating rituals in this species, he does note that the cock is very attentive to his hen during the breeding season.

**MAROON-BELLIED
CONURE**
*Pyrrhura frontalis*

P ODEKERKEN

# MAROON-BELLIED CONURE
## *Pyrrhura frontalis*

### Terminology

The Maroon-bellied Conure *P. frontalis* is also commonly known as the Red-bellied Conure, the Maroon Conure, the Brown-eared Conure and the Scaly-breasted Conure.

### Introduction and Pet Quality

*Maroon-bellied Conure.*

The Maroon-bellied Conure is the all round favourite of conure keepers everywhere. This easily tamed and charming conure makes itself equally comfortable in either its keeper's home or aviary. Judi Robben lists their attributes: 'They are active, playful, full of energy, always into everything, just wonderful.'

Their quietness, according to Robben, makes them an excellent apartment pet. Kam Pelham-Polk confirms that they are quiet, especially when compared to the *Aratinga* species. She admits, however, that they are noisy but the noise is tolerable. Only when absolutely necessary does this species resort to its strong voice to issue warning calls to the flock. Otherwise, it remains relatively silent. Its quietness may account for its lack of ability to mimic human speech and everyday sounds.

However, being quiet does not necessarily mean that this bird is a pushover in the world of parrots. The Maroon-bellied Conure is a feisty conure, which acts aggressively when under threat. Therefore, take care not to startle or frighten this bird. Robben says: 'They will take on any other bird no matter what size – one of my babies went after my Blue and Gold Macaw!'

Pelham-Polk says that there is little, if any, reason for concern over the Maroon-bellied Conure's potential for destructiveness. It does very little chewing on its roost box entrance hole or anything else. However, she does raise one concern about them. 'I find that they make great pets but do need to be handled on a regular daily basis. They do go through a nippy stage and can continue that way if not handled a lot.' This too was Robben's one hesitation. 'They can become nippy if you let them do anything they want. You must be the alpha bird with these birds. Gentle, nurturing dominance is a must.'

Sadly, this all-time favourite is losing ground in the avicultural community, says Pelham-Polk. 'They are conspicuous by their absence.' By all indications, these easily bred conures that she recommends for beginners, are being passed over in favour of the Green-cheeked Conure *P. m. molinae*. This, Pelham-Polk deems as an error. 'I personally have found that the Maroon-bellied Conure makes a sweeter pet. I would like to see more people breed them before we lose them totally.' Robben also recommends them for novice breeders because they are easy to breed.

## Description

Obviously, their popularity is not based on brilliant colouration for this species is best described as being subdued rather than flashy. Its ability to blend with its natural surroundings when viewed from above protects it from the sharp eyes of predators: green head, green back, green wings, which make it invisible against tropical jungle foliage.

However, the appearance is not all camouflage green. When viewed from the front this bird has attractive display markings for communication and mating rituals. This conure fits the characteristic *Pyrrhura* mould, sporting a scalloped bib with matching coloured ear coverts. For added effect, they have a dark beak and darker green face blush that emphasises their white eye rings. Their trademark is the maroon-coloured inner thighs, underbelly and undersides of the tail feathers, which resemble the maroon lining of a green cloak.

Low describes the Maroon-bellied Conure thus: 'It has maroon on the forehead and an irregular patch of that colour on the abdomen. The crown and cheeks are dark green, also the nape, where the feathers have a lighter edge. The ear coverts are light buffish brown. The sides of the neck and the feathers of the upper breast are scalloped in the typical *Pyrrhura* fashion: olive on the breast, edged with yellowish, or exceptionally, golden yellow. The feathers of the sides of the neck are tipped with whitish yellow. The tail feathers are maroon on the under side; the upper surface is green at the base, reddish from the centre to the tip.' The length is approximately 25cm and weight approximately 85 grams.

## In the Wild

The Maroon-bellied Conure ranges through Uruguay, north-eastern Argentina, Paraguay and eastern south-eastern Brazil in South America. It is believed to be common throughout its territory. Joseph Forshaw states that they generally travel in small groups of 10–40 birds. Because of the way they blend so beautifully with the forest canopy and their tendency to be silent during feeding, they have been difficult to study. This quiet behaviour in the wild seems to be common to all the *Pyrrhura* species, and may explain the lack of information we have on their wild behaviour and breeding.

## Breeding

If you can accommodate large numbers of parrot chicks, this conure is for you. 'This species is very prolific,' says Low describing pairs that clutched four times a year and reared as many as five chicks at each outing.

Arndt agrees with Low and gives the Maroon-bellied Conure the prize for representing 'the genus most willing to breed,' and also praises their high fertilisation and hatchout counts. He cautions, however, that parents, on occasion, have been known to ignore one of their chicks. Close nest surveillance is therefore mandatory in case the need arises to pull an ignored chick for handrearing. To avoid disturbing the adults during the brooding of the eggs and while the chicks are being parent raised, clutch inspection should be restricted to those occasions when both adults are absent from the box.

For optimal breeding, Arndt recommends using a nestbox having 20cm square floor space, and that the pair should be housed in an area at least 2 metres long x 1 metre wide x 2 metre high, and never in a box-shaped enclosure.

Bob and Wendy Wilson successfully breed the Maroon-bellied Conure using a cockatiel-sized nestbox – a 35cm cube-shaped box with a 4cm diameter entrance hole. The nestbox is situated at a high point in an accessible yet secluded location of the flight. Pelham-Polk uses a nestbox the same size as that recommended by Arndt. She calls this a lovebird size nestbox. 'Like most conures, they shovel all the bedding out of the box and try to lay on the floor. They sleep in their boxes all year round.' Robben's pairs do the same. 'Mine like to empty the box of shavings so I put more in it as they start to lay... it's all part of the mating ritual to make their nest.'

High fertility rates are certainly the norm for Robben. Her pairs produce 2–4 clutches a year with 6–8 eggs in each clutch. Pelham-Polk's breeding pairs can lay as many as eight eggs per clutch, but four or five are usual. From Robben's and the Wilsons' experience, incubation lasts from 22–24 days and the chicks fledge at approximately 6–7 weeks of age. Robben, however, finds that her chicks hatch with white down whereas the Wilsons insist their chicks have 'very thick grey-coloured down'.

Maroon-bellied Conure in breeding cage at nestbox entrance hole.

Pelham-Polk continues to be alert when within the reach of these conures during its breeding season. 'They are great parents and will become aggressive towards the caregiver to protect their nesting area.' Robben disagrees, saying that her birds are not as aggressive towards their keepers during breeding season as many other conures can be.

If you want your chicks to have top marks as pets, for being tame and having an agreeable character, Pelham-Polk suggests you pull the chicks for handfeeding before their eyes open. To avoid having chicks with a bad attitude, she stresses that the weaned chicks should be housed individually or in pairs.

Robben adds that because they do lay such large clutches, she will often 'foster out the last few eggs that are going to hatch so that the hen will not be overworked. If there are eight chicks in a clutch, the older ones can be 16 days ahead of the youngest ones which then get lost in the box and are not fed. I have had Painted Conures *P. p. picta* hatch Maroon-bellied Conure eggs and feed the young. I just tuck the eggs in anywhere I can if the clutch is really big.'

Arndt's description of mating behaviour is quite fascinating: 'The cock spreads his tail feathers and invites the hen to feed by bowing in an up-and-down motion of the torso. In addition, he spreads his plumage. The hen responds with the same ritual.'

Once fledged, the normal practice in aviculture is to remove parent reared chicks from their parent's range before hostilities occur. However, with this species, Arndt found that the weaned chicks are not chased or injured by the adults, and so may remain with their parents for some time.

**GREEN-CHEEKED
CONURE**
*Pyrrhura molinae molinae*

P ODEKERKEN

# GREEN-CHEEKED CONURE
*Pyrrhura molinae molinae*

## Terminology

The Green-cheeked Conure *P. m. molinae* is also commonly known as the Molina's Conure. This is the common name I prefer as it also refers to the scientific name – the more we use the scientific names, the less ambiguity there will be. After all, have you noticed the large number of conures that have green cheeks?

## Introduction and Pet Quality

What higher praise could any conure want than that of a President of the International Conure Association. 'They are inexpensive and easy to keep and breed, which makes them an ideal aviary bird. They are not very noisy so they are fine in an apartment. Lastly, most handreared babies are very sweet and some even talk. My vote for favourite conure is, of course, the Green-cheeked Conure,' states Sandi Brennan.

Frankly, until Brennan spoke up, we were having serious reservations about being able to make an argument for the Green-cheeked Conure as a companion pet. Everywhere we looked we found cautions. Low, for instance, has quoted owners who have found handreared chicks to be 'very nippy after weaning and unfriendly with birds of other species.' Janet Casagrande confirms that they do go through a nippy or 'beaking' period. Nevertheless, according to her own experience, this problem is remedied with the bird becoming amiable after 'nurturing and proper guidance' through chickhood.

Arndt's evaluation of this species focuses on its aviary compatibility. By looking to his own collection, Arndt assesses them to be enchanting, lively, bath-loving, minimally destructive and cold hardy birds. He adds what one could consider to be the highest praise in terms of conures: 'They are never heard to scream fully, not even when excited.' In addition, he notes that they are extremely peaceful in a communal aviary. Arndt urges us to choose from domestically bred stock whenever possible. Wild birds are naturally timid (no-one wants to see only the backs of their birds as they flee into their nestbox). In addition, he advises offering these birds a wide variety of foods and monitoring their food choices carefully to make sure that their diet does not become too restricted.

Exactly how prolific is this conure? 'In my opinion, Green-cheeked Conures are in no danger of extinction in captivity. In fact, they are so prolific that they are fast becoming as common as cockatiels,' states Brennan.

They are, therefore, readily available. This is encouraging for a species we were at first having a problem defending. Consider their advantages: captivating personality and potential as a companion bird, minimally destructive behaviour and relatively quiet nature for a conure. In addition, they are prolific, easy breeders and offer the opportunity for a communal aviary.

## Description

Imagine the Maroon-bellied Conure *P. frontalis*. Now change the colour of its forehead, crown, nape and upper breast. The upper breast feathers are 'pale brown, sometimes tinged with green, each feather being broadly margined with pale greyish buff or dull yellow and tipped with dark brown.' Low continues: 'The crown and nape are brown, the forehead reddish brown and the cheeks green. The upper side of tail is maroon.' The length is 26cm and weight approximately 90 grams.

It seems to us that Green-cheeked Conures often have more red on their bellies than the Maroon-bellied Conure. The difference is really the dark upper head colour.

## In the Wild

The Green-cheeked Conure is common in its native habitat of the tropical forests of northern and eastern Bolivia, the Mato Grosso area in Brazil, and north-west Argentina. It has been sighted as high up as 2000 metres in the highlands of eastern Bolivia. (It is not surprising, therefore, that they are cold hardy in outdoor aviaries.) Thomas Arndt has found that this forest dweller flies in large swarms amongst the tree tops. Being common, it is ironic that not much else is known of their wild behaviour.

## Breeding

Arndt and Low describe what was probably a first breeding by Swiss aviculturist Dr. Burkard in the early 1970s. Burkard's pair had dug one metre tunnels under the aviary's wooden floorboards. (Mice were no deterrent.) Two chicks were reared in an 'enlarged nesting hollow.' The chicks would flee into tunnels to avoid detection during 'nestbox' inspection: the keeper had to raise the floorboards to check on the young. Natural wonders never cease. (Although this has little relevance to their breeding, it was amazing that when the chicks finally emerged from their catacomb nest, they were greeted by a round of loud cheering shrieks from all the adult birds.) Evidently, these conures can be secretive breeders.

Although the dimensions of the nestboxes were not included, Arndt mentions breeding success using a more traditional nestbox. Five eggs per pair per clutch are considered the norm. On occasion, as many as seven eggs are laid. However seven eggs do not necessarily mean seven chicks, cautions Arndt. The fertility rate can fluctuate considerably between breeding pairs. Robben advises that incubation lasts approximately 22 days and that the chicks hatch with white down and fledge at approximately 6–7 weeks of age.

*Green-cheeked Conures*

Arndt points out that when given the choice between a tree cavity and a nestbox, to roost and/or nest in, this conure does not necessarily choose the artificial nestbox first.

This species is considered prolific and can produce up to three clutches per year, says Brennan. 'Almost all of my pairs have three clutches a year if I take the babies for handrearing by the time the oldest is two to three weeks of age.' For individual pairs she uses both a 25cm square x 35cm deep box and a mini boot that is 20cm square x 35cm high and 35cm deep at the foot.

Adult birds have been found to be good parents, so there are few in-nest chick fatalities. (However, it is always good practice to monitor the nestbox.)

A communal aviary housing numerous pairs of Green-cheeked Conures was studied by Arndt. He found that even when each pair had been provided with their own roosting site, all the birds would cram into just one site anyway. Even when pairs were nesting, they roosted communally. However, if sleeping quarters are too close, egg breakage is inevitable. Perhaps an apartment block sized nestbox is called for when housing a flock communally!

*Above and right:*
*Pair of Green-cheeked Conures.*

*Below:*
*Green-cheeked conure chicks in nest box.*

**CRIMSON-BELLIED CONURE**
*Pyrrhura perlata perlata*

P ODEKERKEN

# CRIMSON-BELLIED CONURE
## *Pyrrhura perlata perlata*

### Terminology

The Crimson-bellied Conure *P. p. perlata* is also commonly known as the Crimson-breasted Conure. Some aviculturists incorrectly call this species the Pearly Conure. In actual fact the Pearly Conure is now considered to be *P. p. lepida*. Previously the Crimson-bellied Conure was referred to as *P. rhodogaster*.

### Introduction and Pet Quality

The Crimson-bellied Conure is described by Low as one of the most beautiful of all conures. Low, however, also ranks this conure as one of the rarest of all conures in aviculture.

Because they are rare and thus precious, Arndt suggests that the owner take special care when acclimatising this bird to its new home. They are naturally shy birds, so they may be skittish at first, but will soon calm down and may even become tame. As they are fliers with a strong need to exercise, Arndt urges the owner to provide their birds

*Handreared Crimson-bellied Conure.*

with a generously sized flight. (He also describes them as bath loving birds, so a bird bath and a regular bath time is also a necessity.)

Regarding their potential for destructiveness, Arndt says that it varies with the individual bird. Any potential they may have for wood gnawing can be diverted by offering them an abundant and constant supply of fresh twigs and branches upon which to chew. This should distract them from the tempting timber surfaces of their nestbox and of the aviary structure.

As for their loudness, Arndt comments that they rarely use their full voice, and usually only when excited or startled. Their voice is actually considered agreeable to the ear. They also have their own unique and extensive repertoire of calls.

Arndt also reports that the Crimson-bellied Conure exhibits a strong flocking instinct. As an example of this, he cites an instance when birds escaped from their aviary but returned in the evening to the flock (and so were easily recaptured).

Rick Jordan takes his admiration for the Crimson-bellied Conure a step further than Low by declaring it to be 'probably one of the most beautiful birds on the face of the earth,' and describes this species as being 'inquisitive without being 'pushy' or 'nippy'.' Jordan believes that the Crimson-bellied Conure is probably one of the quietest of all conure species. They do get excited and 'chatter' if someone approaches them and they are in a breeding situation. However, a single pet is basically very quiet. The domestic birds that he works with do not destroy wood. He mentions one notable peculiarity. Young birds will often sleep 'lying down' if they do not have a perch in the weaning cage. He has even caught them sleeping upside down on their heads in the corners of their brooders. Often he has thought they were dead and gone running to the brooder only to have them stand up and beg for food.

As for the birds' tolerance of the cold, Jordan houses his pairs outdoors, all year round in Texas. 'We do get some cold nights,' he adds 'sometimes with temperatures dipping below freezing for a few days in a row. They seem to cope with the cold and have shown no stress or illness because of it. Most pairs do not even sleep in the nestbox until breeding season approaches. Of course there are exceptions to that rule and some pairs will immediately move into the nestbox at night.'

## Description

Rosemary Low describes this species thus: 'In the Crimson-bellied Conure, the whole of the lower parts from the upper breast to the vent are brilliant scarlet. The cheeks are yellowish green and blue. The feathers of the crown, nape, sides of neck, throat and upper breast are brown with a paler tip, giving a barred appearance. There is a variable blue collar surrounding the hind neck. The bend of the wing and the underwing coverts are crimson. The median wing coverts, thighs, flanks and undertail coverts are blue. The tail is brownish red, marked with green at the base and tipped with blue above and greyish below. The bill is brownish grey and the iris dark brown.' The length is 24cm and the weight is approximately 75–85 grams.

## In the Wild

The Crimson-bellied Conure resides in the rainforest canopy of northern Brazil, just below the Equator, south of the Amazon River in South America. Only on rare occasions are these conures ever sighted in their native habitat between the Madeira and Tapajós Rivers. Very little is known of their wild behaviour except that they gather in the canopies of the lowland trees. In 1916, an expedition saw this species forming in large swarms amongst trees along river banks.

Joseph Forshaw and Thomas Arndt both relate Cherrie's 1916 experience in the northern Mato Grosso area of Brazil. Cherrie found that, when undisturbed and totally at ease in their environment, this species constantly chattered amongst themselves and fluttered about in the trees. However, they were constantly on the alert for danger. When startled or alarmed, instead of taking flight, they froze and, even with their brightly coloured feathers, became almost invisible. They use the shield provided by silence and camouflage to avoid the sharp eyes of their predators. (Anyone who has attempted to approach a flock of birds undetected will tell you that this is next to impossible. It seems possible, therefore, that someone could be standing in the midst of a large swarm of these stealth birds and be totally unaware of their presence. It is no wonder that they are so rarely seen in the wild.)

In the late 1970s, these conures were observed gathered in small flocks of three to eight individuals. They kept to the dense foliage of the tropical forest trees and were seen eating fruits and blossoms.

# Breeding

When selecting a breeding pair Arndt suggests having the birds sexed. When these conures form pairs on their own, same sex partners are not unusual. One bird assumes the role of the missing sex partner for courtship rituals and mating.

Interestingly, Arndt found that when offered the choice between a nestbox measuring 21cm square x 30cm high and a tree trunk, the birds chose the nestbox. A detectable change in the behaviour of each member of the pair heralds the start of the breeding season. The cock becomes shy, retreating to the nestbox when sensing danger; the hen becomes aggressive, in defence of her nest. Clutches consist of approximately five eggs of which the breeder should count on only two or three being fertile.

ABK

*Above: Crimson-bellied Conure on nestbox.*
*Below: Two Crimson-bellied Conure chicks with a Maroon-bellied Conure chick.*

Rick Jordan recommends the Crimson-bellied Conure for the hobby breeder as easy to keep, quiet, and fairly easy to breed. His only qualification is that this species can be very determined when they are set up for breeding. In other words, they want to be where they want to be and they want to be fed when they want to be fed. They are fearless and many are not even afraid of a bird catching net or a pair of gloved hands.

Jordan offers these breeding tips: 'This species appears to be one of the easier to breed. It helps if they are not placed

directly beside larger Psittacines that may intimidate them, although not much intimidates them! They do well in pairs set up close to each other, and best when separated from all other *Pyrrhura* species. Once they become accustomed to their cage and their neighbouring birds, nothing seems to bother them.'

His pairs are housed in medium-sized cages designed for *Pyrrhura* conures measuring 61–76cm wide x 61–91.5cm high x 1.5 metres long. Each cage has two perches, one positioned low at the front and one positioned high at the back so that the birds can fly from one to the other if they please. The nestbox measures 28cm square x 46cm deep. A 5cm entrance hole is placed near the top front and a wire ladder is placed inside the box so the birds can descend safely into the nestbox. The nestbox is positioned near the top of the cage at either the food end or the opposite end of the cage. Both setups have worked and resulted in breeding. For nestbox substrate, Jordan uses clean, untreated pine shavings, and finds that the birds do not toss it out. He has also used large, chunky cypress mulch in the boxes with success.

Jordan's Crimson-bellied Conures may lay up to four clutches of 3–6 eggs per season commencing in early winter. Often the first clutches appear in freezing weather and therefore some of the eggs may be lost if the hen does not sit tightly. During cold weather the eggs are removed and the chicks are hatched in a hatcher as the hen cannot properly brood several larger chicks at one time. The incubation period is 23 days. The chicks hatch with slight, mostly white down. Hatch weight is 5–7 grams. Handfeeding is usually uneventful and chicks often wean at about six weeks of age. At weaning they do not display the full crimson colour on the belly as seen in the adult plumage. The fledgling period is 36–45 days. Adult plumage appears at different ages, in some at six months of age, in others at 9–12 months of age.

Jordan says that his handraised chicks will breed successfully at eight months of age if they are introduced to proven breeders. Two handraised birds housed together often take about one year or slightly longer to mature and to begin laying fertile eggs. Jordan feels that the birds are fairly reliable parents, even if handraised. He comments, 'As a matter of fact, it is the parent reared birds that are often too nervous to attempt nesting and are more prone to damage eggs or chicks in the nest.'

'Chicks left with the parents for longer than six months may get 'picked on' or 'plucked' by the parent birds,' cautions Jordan. 'It is best to keep the babies in small groups until you decide to set them up for breeding.'

Jordan describes the courtship rituals thus: 'Cocks court hens much like other *Pyrrhura* conures. The cock will approach the hen on the perch while bobbing the head slightly and raising the 'hackles' on his neck. He will feed her and mate with her if she is receptive. They often then retreat to the nestbox where you can hear them verbalising and possibly mating again.'

P ODEKERKEN

*Pair of Crimson-bellied Conures.*

**PAINTED CONURE**
*Pyrrhura picta picta*

# PAINTED CONURE
## *Pyrrhura picta picta*

## Terminology

According to Forshaw, *P. p. picta* is the nominate of the nine recognised subspecies of the Painted Conure. The word *picta* is from the Latin and means 'a painting', hence the English common name, the Painted Conure. This species is also known commonly as the Blue-winged Conure.

## Introduction and Pet Quality

Low describes the Painted Conure as a 'most attractively marked bird.' In spite of its beauty and although fairly common in the wild, for some reason this conure seems to be resisting popularity and remains uncommon in aviculture.

This bird's rarity in captivity may be due to conflicting impressions about its nature, revealing the danger of making generalisations. Arndt reports that what he has heard, for example, raises questions on their suitability as a pet or aviary bird. He notes that some people have found them to be very nervous and difficult to tame, whereas others he spoke to have found these conures very trusting and attached to their keeper. (The difference here may be between the nervous, wild-caught and the calm, tame, handraised bird.) Even Brennan admits to never having had much success with them. 'The few I handreared were nippy until weaned then stayed pleasant as long as they were played with on a regular basis.'

On the other hand, Robben is 'addicted' to these conures. 'I love the Painted Conure. It is probably my favourite conure and yes, you may quote me on that.' Robben's unqualified enthusiasm was surprising in light of all the contradictory literature on this species. She explains her attraction to these birds: 'They have that 'big bird' personality: active, outgoing and inquisitive. They don't seem to be as aggressive and nippy as the Green-cheeked *P. m. molinae* and Maroon-bellied Conures *P. frontalis* that I raise... and their beauty... such wonderful colour and even more so as they mature. If handfed and well-socialised, they make wonderful, loving and well-interacting pets.'

With regard to that infamous conure trait of loudness, Robben does not consider them loud at all. However, she shrugs, 'of course I have mini macaws and a lot of *Aratingas*.' Robben also does not consider them to be destructive. 'The nestbox may get a bit of chewing but very little. Toys are fair game but they don't seem to destroy them.'

Robben does admit that Painted Conures should be handled daily to prevent them from becoming nippy and aggressive.

Because of the unbalanced ratio of cocks to hens of this species in the USA, Robben recommends that breeders only sell cocks as pets, retaining the hens to sell to other breeders.

Robben has set up each cage with several perches of different sizes, a swing and toys. A nestbox is attached to the outside of the cage.

Usually, only wild-caught birds are available. To help them overcome their shyness, Arndt advises that these birds should be provided with a large spacious flight. Some imported birds, however, never did tame down and remained restless and easily excited whenever changes occurred in their environment.

With regard to outdoor aviaries, Arndt recommends acclimatising birds to inside temperatures before housing them outdoors. They can become hardy to light frost temperatures in a sheltered outdoor aviary provided, of course, that they have access to a warm roosting box. (Low also speaks of how cold hardy they are as long as they have access to a frost-free shelter with a nestbox.) Their cold hardiness is surprising considering their proximity to the Equator in their wild habitat.

What are the special needs of the Painted Conure? Provide them with fresh branches daily, such as apple and pear branches, advises Arndt. Willow and eucalyptus branches can also be safely used. Another need is for a bath. Arndt describes this species as being extremely fond of bathing. (Robben also finds this to be the case.)

As for their behaviour, as mentioned previously, you really cannot generalise about their character. Arndt's experience is that some are quiet and trusting whereas others are lively. On a rare occasion, they were even found to be fearful. Equally unpredictable is their love for bathing, covering the spectrum from the timid bather to the avid frolicker. As gnawers, Arndt places them in the category of mild, but with the odd exception falling into the depraved destruction category. As for quietness, Arndt ranked this conure as being quiet with only the rare outburst, as might be expected. The only caution cast by Arndt is in regard to their tendency to cling onto the aviary wire walls – their tail feathers take a beating. Unfortunately, no remedy is offered.

P ODEKERKEN

*Painted Conure.*

## Description

Low describes the Painted Conure thus: 'It has the crown and nape dark brown, suffused with blue on the crown in most of the subspecies recognised. There is blue on the lower cheeks and hind neck. The lores and the upper cheeks are maroon and the ear coverts are pale buff. The feathers of the neck, throat and upper breast are dusky brown or green, broadly edged with greyish buff to give the usual scalloped effect, but these light markings are V-shaped, not following the contour of the feathers as in other *Pyrrhura* species. There is a maroon patch from the lower back to the uppertail coverts and another on the abdomen. The bend of the wing is green with red-tipped feathers. The tail is maroon above, coppery red below.' The length is 22cm and weight is approximately 55 grams.

## In the Wild

The Painted Conure resides in Venezuela (south of the Orinoco River), Guyana, Surinam and French Guiana as well as in northern Brazil, South America. Rosemary Low deems it to be common 'over much of its range.'

Arndt's findings differ from Low's. He states that this species is only common in Surinam, living in swarms in the forests and coastal regions. They flock only in small groups in the forests on the higher mountain slopes. He says that they are quiet only when feeding.

# Breeding

Robben conducted a poll of fellow Painted Conure owners. The consensus was that these conures are 'sporadic' breeders. 'We had 47 pairs set up for breeding, all were mature and able to breed. Of those 47 pairs, only three pairs actually produced in 1998. These are not good odds.'

In spite of the potential for low breeding results, Robben is enthusiastic about breeding this conure. When she started out, unrelated young handfed chicks were obtained for eventual breeding stock. This has proved beneficial. 'This didn't start as a thought out process, but actually has been one of the wisest things I have done. I now prefer those domestic handraised birds for breeders. They seem to be steadier breeders and don't mind my interference in their lives. Nestbox checks are not stressful when the parents are comfortable with the aviculturist.'

Robben's breeding pairs are housed as individual pairs in an indoor facility complete with timer-controlled, full spectrum lighting. The breeding cages measure 1.2 metres long x 76cm wide x 61cm high and are two-tiered. The corridors between the cages have plants to block the view of shy birds as well as to give the aviary a jungle-like environment. 'For pairs that are reserved in nature, I have put up some natural coloured hessian as a barrier but I don't know that it really helps. To be honest, I just give them time to produce and if they don't then I make gradual changes with things such as cage location, mates, barriers and boxes.'

Each breeding pair is offered a variety of nestboxes, until one is accepted. Robben's first producing pair used a cockatiel box measuring 23cm square x 30cm high, the second chose a boot-shaped box measuring 20cm square x 56cm high, and the third pair a rectangular box measuring 25cm square x 30cm long. 'I just keep changing until I find something they prefer. Most breeders are calling for grandfather clock-shaped nestboxes now and say that the smaller and tighter the boxes are, the better they are accepted. Once accepted, the pair uses the box to nest as well as to roost in year round. Small, dark and tight seems best.' The boxes are attached onto the upper exterior section of the cage.

Robben decides on the bird pairings and then monitors them for compatibility. 'If they don't eat side by side, sleep in the box together and regurgitate for each other then I will re-pair them. My pairs are fairly aggressive when they are in breeding mode. Hens sit so

J ROBBEN

*Painted Conure guarding eggs.*

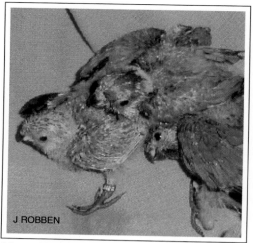

J ROBBEN

*Young Painted Conure chicks.*

tightly on their eggs that it is hard to get to them to candle them and to check on chicks. I usually get two clutches a year from them, and I pull babies at approximately 2–3 weeks for handfeeding. They usually wean at approximately 6–7 weeks of age. Once they start flying well they wean very fast.' Her chicks hatch with white down after 21–23 days of incubation.

When asked if anything else is done specially for breeding Painted Conures, Robben added: 'All cages have a small cement [mineral stone] perch near the box where the cock sits when the hen is incubating. [The cement perch helps trim nails which keeps them from puncturing eggs during incubation.] It is a favourite perch location while breeding [copulating] as it is sturdy and easy to perch on. I also have perches made of natural wood of varying widths and lengths on each end of the cage so they can fly about from perch to perch in the cages.'

As mentioned by Robben, Arndt also issues a warning about the aggressive behaviour of the Painted Conure during the breeding season. Arndt advises housing breeding pairs individually in a flight measuring 3 metres long x 1 metre wide x 2 metres high. To cater for possible winter breeding, a nestbox measuring 25cm square x 35cm high with a 7.5cm diameter entrance hole should be adequate enough to insulate the eggs from cooling.

Interestingly, Arndt has found that breeding pairs often prefer a cave to a nestbox. Unfortunately, the dimensions of the cave are not given. However, Arndt does describe copulation as lasting two or three minutes and accompanied 'by impressive, noisy utterances resembling humming groans.' Contrary to Robben's observations, Arndt cites that the cock remains in the nestbox with the hen during incubation – a rarity with *Pyrrhura* species.

# AFTERTHOUGHTS

## Carry the Conure Flame!

Once you fall in love with conures, you will be hooked. Mark my words! Conure keeping is habit-forming and quickly becomes an addiction. You start with one, then you get another and then you start breeding them. Soon you find yourself belonging to conure associations and parrot clubs. You will even find yourself at the big events of aviculture, the parrot symposiums, conventions and exhibitions. You will become involved locally and eventually globally. This is exactly what happened to Glenn Reynolds, primary fund-raiser for the World Parrot Trust-USA Golden Conure Survival Fund.

Reynolds became interested in breeding the Queen of Bavaria's (Golden) Conure *G. guarouba* because of its rarity, and then went on to become involved in fund-raising for a field study of this species. His experience is typical of a dedicated aviculturist: 'I have been a bird owner for over 22 years. I started breeding small birds, primarily cockatiels,

15 years ago. I learned the ropes and soon moved on to larger birds. I have bred Sun Conures [*A. solstitialis*] in the past, which started my affection for the conures. About the same time that I became interested in conures, I was also shifting my interests to the breeding of rarer birds. I felt that it was time that I gave something back to aviculture. I bought some Palm Cockatoos, Hyacinthine Macaws, Red-fronted Macaws and Queen of Bavaria's Conures. It was not quite as easy and quick as that statement makes it sound. I second-mortgaged my house for my first Palm Cockatoo and found a financial partner for the second one. I purchased baby Hyacinthine Macaw chicks and finished handraising them for resale to learn about them and to raise the money to purchase a pair. Before I actually bought a pair, I was sent a pair on breeder loan. I also have a partner on the Queen of Bavaria's Conures, and I purchased the Red-fronted Macaws outright. Arranging the permit for the Queen of Bavaria's Conure was an education in itself. I am just an average guy who has a passion for birds (especially the rare ones). Once I owned these rarer birds I wanted to know how I could help them. That is when I talked with Mike Reynolds (Founder and Chairman of the World Parrot Trust) about doing a project for the Queen of Bavaria's Conures, and decided to adopt it as my responsibility.'

Your help is needed in a number of areas of aviculture. For example, the study of conures in captivity is but in its infancy. Much needs to be learned, recorded and shared. Why must the novice conure keeper have to rely on 'trial and error' methods and thus place his/her conures and their potential chicks at risk? Those with experience are urged to share their knowledge and methods, for the betterment of all conure-kind. Aviculture is very much an oral tradition, so share your findings with fellow members at conure associations and parrot clubs. Contribute to their bulletins and newsletters. Volunteer your time. Become involved.

A plea to conure breeders who can accommodate an extra pair or two: many conure species are on the brink of extinction in the wild and therefore must establish a toehold in captive breeding or disappear altogether. Housing and breeding such birds is more an act of charity than a moneymaking proposition, more for the sake of preserving the conure gene pool and supplying rare chicks to other breeders. Such species need a lot of help if they are ever to achieve sufficient numbers to warrant entry into the pet trade. Support field study programs. As you will have noted throughout the species section of this book, our repeated comment was 'little is known of their behaviour in the wild.' This need not be the case in future editions of this book. Consider assisting the conservation of conures in the wild. 'I don't understand why most bird owners refuse to get involved in conservation,' laments Glenn Reynolds. 'They don't realise that just five dollars will go a long way. If every bird owner would donate five dollars to conservation, we could save most of the parrots.' Since March 1999, Reynolds has been 'consumed' by fundraising for the Golden Conure Survival Fund.

## Useful Web Sites and Addresses

members.nbci.com/iconurea/index.html — For information or membership regarding the International Conure Association. Or contact Teri Bilbe, PO Box 60053, Corpus Christi, Texas, USA, 78466.

pyrrhurabreedersassocaition.hypermart.net — To support and join the Pyrrhura Breeders Association. Or write to them at PO Box 621, Goddard, Kansas, USA, 67052.

www.aratingaclub.com/ — For information on the Aratinga Conures.

www.parrotsociety.org.au — Parrot Society of Australia Inc. Or write to PO Box 75, Salisbury, Queensland 4107, Australia.

www.thegabrielfoundation.org — The Gabriel Foundation is a non-profit organisation promoting education, rescue, rehabilitation, adoption and sanctuary for companion parrots. Or write to PO Box 11477, Aspen, Colorado, USA, 81612.

www.worldparrottrust.org — Help save the parrots of the world by joining The World Parrot Trust.

# BIBLIOGRAPHY AND RECOMMENDED READING

Before interviewing conure owners and breeders for their personal experiences, we gathered basic information about conures from published sources.

Arndt, T. 1993, *Atlas of Conures: Aratingas and Pyrrhuras*, translated by A. Lambrich, TFH Publications, New Jersey.

> This is one of the most expansive published sources on conures. Much of the work is still current, and the book is a valuable resource. Arndt's own beautiful watercolours illustrate the text. Like Forshaw, he provides maps showing where the birds are found in the wild. Unfortunately, as the title depicts, this book only covers the *Aratinga* and *Pyrrhura* species.

Forshaw, J. M., *Parrots of the World*, 3rd edn., rev., Lansdowne Editions, Australia.

> This is an excellent all-round volume in which Forshaw not only describes the conures, but has also compiled historical references to the birds in the wild. He also provides a map noting the distribution of each species. The illustrations by William T. Cooper are beautiful (if not perfectly accurate).

Kremer, H. 1992, *Aratingas*, Noordbergum: Ornis.

> We also consulted this volume extensively. One of the most fascinating aspects of Kremer's book is his use of notations on the meaning of many of the scientific names. His text gives descriptions of each species of *Aratinga*, with information on wild habits as well as avicultural details on breeding. Like Forshaw and Arndt, he provides maps illustrating the species' range in South America. Unfortunately Kremer has not done the same for the other genus of conures.

Low, R. 1992, *Parrots: Their Care and Breeding*, 3rd edn., Blandford Press, London.

> This text was an obvious place to start. Low describes each species of conure from the point of view of physical appearance, native range, and, in most cases, also offers an overview of its avicultural record. Photographs illustrate the book, although not all species are represented visually. Nevertheless, this is an excellent reference book.

Other useful references:

Cannon, Dr M. J. 1996, *A Guide to Basic Health and Disease in Birds*, ABK Publications.

Digney, P. 1998, *A Guide to Incubation and Handraising Parrots*, ABK Publications.

Dorge, R. & Sibley, G 1998, *A Guide to Pet and Companion Birds,* ABK Publications.

> Our book provides an overview on parrot keeping basics and offers an introduction to understanding your parrot's behaviour.

Martin, Dr T., *A Guide to Genetics and Colour Mutations in Parrots*, ABK Publications, to be released late 2001.

*Handbook of Birds, Cages and Aviaries*, 1997, ABK Publications.